Sigmund Freud

Titles in the series Critical Lives present the work of leading cultural figures of the modern period. Each book explores the life of the artist, writer, philosopher or architect in question and relates it to their major works.

In the same series

Hannah Arendt *Samantha Rose Hill*
Antonin Artaud *David A. Shafer*
Roland Barthes *Andy Stafford*
Georges Bataille *Stuart Kendall*
Charles Baudelaire *Rosemary Lloyd*
Simone de Beauvoir *Ursula Tidd*
Samuel Beckett *Andrew Gibson*
Walter Benjamin *Esther Leslie*
John Berger *Andy Merrifield*
Leonard Bernstein *Paul R. Laird*
Joseph Beuys *Claudia Mesch*
Jorge Luis Borges *Jason Wilson*
Constantin Brancusi *Sanda Miller*
Bertolt Brecht *Philip Glahn*
Charles Bukowski *David Stephen Calonne*
Mikhail Bulgakov *J.A.E. Curtis*
William S. Burroughs *Phil Baker*
John Cage *Rob Haskins*
Albert Camus *Edward J. Hughes*
Fidel Castro *Nick Caistor*
Paul Cézanne *Jon Kear*
Coco Chanel *Linda Simon*
Noam Chomsky *Wolfgang B. Sperlich*
Jean Cocteau *James S. Williams*
Joseph Conrad *Robert Hampson*
Salvador Dalí *Mary Ann Caws*
Charles Darwin *J. David Archibald*
Guy Debord *Andy Merrifield*
Claude Debussy *David J. Code*
Gilles Deleuze *Frida Beckman*
Fyodor Dostoevsky *Robert Bird*
Marcel Duchamp *Caroline Cros*
Sergei Eisenstein *Mike O'Mahony*
William Faulkner *Kirk Curnutt*
Gustave Flaubert *Anne Green*
Michel Foucault *David Macey*
Benjamin Franklin *Kevin J. Hayes*
Sigmund Freud *Matt ffytche*
Mahatma Gandhi *Douglas Allen*
Jean Genet *Stephen Barber*
Allen Ginsberg *Steve Finbow*
Johann Wolfgang von Goethe *Jeremy Adler*
Günter Grass *Julian Preece*
Ernest Hemingway *Verna Kale*
Langston Hughes *W. Jason Miller*
Victor Hugo *Bradley Stephens*
Aldous Huxley *Jake Poller*
Derek Jarman *Michael Charlesworth*
Alfred Jarry *Jill Fell*
James Joyce *Andrew Gibson*
Carl Jung *Paul Bishop*
Franz Kafka *Sander L. Gilman*
Frida Kahlo *Gannit Ankori*

Søren Kierkegaard *Alastair Hannay*
Yves Klein *Nuit Banai*
Arthur Koestler *Edward Saunders*
Akira Kurosawa *Peter Wild*
Lenin *Lars T. Lih*
Jack London *Kenneth K. Brandt*
Pierre Loti *Richard M. Berrong*
Rosa Luxemburg *Dana Mills*
Jean-François Lyotard *Kiff Bamford*
René Magritte *Patricia Allmer*
Stéphane Mallarmé *Roger Pearson*
Thomas Mann *Herbert Lehnert and Eva Wessell*
Gabriel García Márquez *Stephen M. Hart*
Karl Marx *Paul Thomas*
Henri Matisse *Kathryn Brown*
Guy de Maupassant *Christopher Lloyd*
Herman Melville *Kevin J. Hayes*
Henry Miller *David Stephen Calonne*
Yukio Mishima *Damian Flanagan*
Eadweard Muybridge *Marta Braun*
Vladimir Nabokov *Barbara Wyllie*
Pablo Neruda *Dominic Moran*
Georgia O'Keeffe *Nancy J. Scott*
Octavio Paz *Nick Caistor*
Pablo Picasso *Mary Ann Caws*
Edgar Allan Poe *Kevin J. Hayes*
Ezra Pound *Alec Marsh*
Marcel Proust *Adam Watt*
Sergei Rachmaninoff *Rebecca Mitchell*
Arthur Rimbaud *Seth Whidden*
John Ruskin *Andrew Ballantyne*
Jean-Paul Sartre *Andrew Leak*
Erik Satie *Mary E. Davis*
Arnold Schoenberg *Mark Berry*
Arthur Schopenhauer *Peter B. Lewis*
Dmitry Shostakovich *Pauline Fairclough*
Adam Smith *Jonathan Conlin*
Susan Sontag *Jerome Boyd Maunsell*
Gertrude Stein *Lucy Daniel*
Stendhal *Francesco Manzini*
Igor Stravinsky *Jonathan Cross*
Rabindranath Tagore *Bashabi Fraser*
Pyotr Tchaikovsky *Philip Ross Bullock*
Leo Tolstoy *Andrei Zorin*
Leon Trotsky *Paul Le Blanc*
Mark Twain *Kevin J. Hayes*
Richard Wagner *Raymond Furness*
Alfred Russel Wallace *Patrick Armstrong*
Simone Weil *Palle Yourgrau*
Tennessee Williams *Paul Ibell*
Ludwig Wittgenstein *Edward Kanterian*
Virginia Woolf *Ira Nadel*
Frank Lloyd Wright *Robert McCarter*

Sigmund Freud

Matt ffytche

REAKTION BOOKS

For A – to those who dream the objects, and those who read them

Published by
REAKTION BOOKS LTD
Unit 32, Waterside
44–48 Wharf Road
London N1 7UX, UK
www.reaktionbooks.co.uk

First published 2022
Copyright © Matt ffytche 2022

Printed and bound in Great Britain by TJ Books Ltd, Padstow, Cornwall

A catalogue record for this book is available from the British Library

ISBN 978 1 78914 579 3

Contents

Sigmund Freud, 1920.

Introduction: The Freudian Aftershock

In September 1907 an eager new recruit to the psychoanalytic movement, the Swiss psychiatrist Carl Jung, wrote to Sigmund Freud expressing a long-cherished wish for a photograph: 'I feel the want of your picture.' Freud complied, but equivocally: 'please, don't make too much of me. I am too human to deserve it.'[1] He detested the picture, which had been taken recently for the Hygiene Exhibition, and preferred instead to send something less artificial, taken by his boys. In the years that followed this encounter Freud was photographed – and indeed painted, etched and sculpted – innumerable times, often by his son-in-law, the photographer Max Halberstadt, sometimes with his famously imposing stare, sometimes captured in a more informal family snapshot. Even during his lifetime the photographs and cartoons proliferated. His was a face that adorned the cover of *Time* magazine as its pin-up in 1924, 1939, 1956 and 1993. It was a face that Freud felt had been charmingly idealized in a 1914 etching by Hermann Struck, but which in a different episode – mirrored accidentally in a swinging bathroom-cabinet door on a train – he mistook for an intruder ('I can still recollect that I thoroughly disliked his appearance').[2] It is also a face into which, during the last sixteen years of his life, he had to insert an uncomfortable prosthesis following surgery for cancer that removed a large part of his upper jaw and palate on the right-hand side – the insert, named 'the monster', pained him immeasurably and hampered his speech and hearing.

What remains attached to this face? In his notes towards a book project left unfinished at his death in 2015, the historian John Forrester set it at the heart of the twentieth century – the 'Freudian Century' – in which individuals in societies all over the globe learned to speak Freudian, to dream Freudian dreams, to make Freudian slips, to have a neurosis, to free associate and to endlessly re-evaluate their mothers and fathers. This was a century in which people learnt to love their symptoms, their traumas, their drives and their unconscious, and to tell many, many Freudian jokes; a century in which psychoanalysis was variously named as the medical branch of science fiction and the philosophy of revolution.[3] Narcissism, projection, sublimation, repression, ambivalence – Freud wasn't in each case the originator of these terms, but psychoanalysis galvanized their introduction into twentieth-century psychology, sustained their application in clinical treatments, and disseminated them through the culture at large. For Freud's detractors – and there have been many – he is Freud the fraud, and his work is 'mental masturbation', a 'psychic-sexual infection' or 'a hellish spook from a brain mythology', something for the credulous and the vulgar.[4]

Of the many death knells that have been sounded for psychoanalysis, none was more devasting than the traumatic exodus of Jewish psychoanalysts from Central Europe during the Nazi years and their relocation to the Americas, Britain (where Freud himself fled), Palestine and elsewhere. They became refugees whose families were murdered, who had lost their institutions, their culture and possessions, and who had to begin connecting the pieces of the psychoanalytic project afresh in alien surroundings. Since then psychoanalysis has survived displacement from its hegemonic position in American psychiatry during the 1950s and '60s by pharmacology and neurobiology; it has survived the 'Freud

Wars' of the 1980s, in which Freud was accused of supplanting evidence of child abuse with his psychology of 'fantasy'; it has survived feminist attacks and the anti-psychiatry movement, and defunding from healthcare organizations in favour of more short-term affordable treatments. In doing so, it has travelled far beyond its place and time of origin to become part of many different cultures and initiatives, be they therapeutic, social, political or intellectual. There has been a Freud for 1920s Bengal and 1930s Tokyo; a Freud for the early days of the Bolshevik revolution and for modernist poets; a Freud for apartheid South Africa; a Freud for the 'years of lead' under Brazilian dictatorship; a Freud for French existentialist philosophy and for Algerian decolonization; a Freud for Zionism and for the '68 student movement in Italy. There has been a Freud for the American 'culture of narcissism' in the 1970s; for Iraqi sociology of the 1950s; and for post-millennium China. His thought has recurred in the Marxist and anti-fascist work of Wilhelm Reich; in Donald Winnicott's war-time radio broadcasts to British mothers and in social care and anti-racist activism in Harlem in the 1940s; in American neo-conservatism and in the cultural anthropology of Margaret Mead; in debates within West German gay communities in the 1970s; in film theory and British cultural studies of the 1980s; in Derridean deconstruction and the gender theory of Judith Butler; in trauma theories of the 1990s; and today in Afropessimism, neuropsychoanalysis, queer theory and ecology, but also of course in contemporary psychotherapies, social work, counselling, nursing and early years pedagogy.

Psychoanalysis has often presented itself as a discipline of the past – a kind of mental archaeology. There is no doubt, too, that Freud's life intersects with many dramatic topics in late Victorian and early twentieth-century history: fin-de-siècle culture in Vienna; the female hysteric and the birth of modern psychology; the revolution in modern sexuality; the impact of the First World War on the ideals of Western culture; the rise of fascism and antisemitism in Central Europe – all of which will be covered here. But it is not itself *of the past*. We are still experiencing the aftershock of Freud's work: we live and breathe in a universe indelibly shaped by Freudian concerns. Today – perhaps more than ever, with the increasing spread of anxieties about mental health, shifting frameworks of social identity, a calling to account of the history of racism and colonialism, and an ongoing probing of the nature of subjective life – Freudian and post-Freudian perspectives not only recur, in the need for talking therapies, but continue to knot themselves into developments in the social sciences and humanities as they reinvent paradigms for living that are appropriate to twenty-first-century crises.

So there is ever a rationale to return to Freud, to tell his story and that of the origins of psychoanalysis. Freud's story is not quite fixed, because we are still deciding what to do with him. But it is not my intention here simply to wrap up the complexity of the contemporary world by slapping on it the dated portrait of a historic white male scientist, as if in another iteration of his *Time* covers. Psychoanalysis has become too protean, too collective, for that. Instead, throughout this volume I will seek to bring out in Freud's work the features that I think continue to justify the existence of psychoanalysis as a necessity. This means more than the perennial popular interest in the meaning of dreams and myths, the nature of sexuality, the experience of anxiety and nervous illness in modern life, and the power of unconscious thoughts and desires, which will all also be considered here. It means, in particular, that – as with atoms, history and society – our 'I' is not a unity. There is no single, simple face to the mental life we claim as our own or call our ego, our consciousness, our identity. Our reality, our subjective reality, and that of others, is never quite where we want to place it, or how we intend to live it. It turns out to be a construction, a displacement, a mechanism for successfully avoiding ourselves. There is no other science that has spawned quite Freud's method, and quite this acute perspective on mental life, or an active global professional body to explore just this question: what it is that individuals or groups functionally conceal from themselves, even – or perhaps especially – when this touches on the most intimate, emotional experiences and the most passionate attachments.

This book is dedicated to the many contemporary scholars – Shaul Bar-Haim, Dagmar Herzog, Carolyn Laubender, George Makari, David Marriott, Andreas Mayer, Stefania Pandolfo, Daniel Pick, Camille Robcis, Joanna Ryan, Raluca Soreanu, Eli Zaretsky, and all those unknown to me – who are helping to render Freud and psychoanalysis anew for the twenty-first century: to produce a Freud beyond patriarchy, beyond colonialism, beyond heterosexuality and gender inequality, beyond privilege. Not as an idealization, but as a point of critical leverage. Many of their works are listed in the Further Reading section, and some are yet to be published. This book draws significantly on this recent scholarship, and if it takes us some of the way to a Freud who is useful and relevant for making sense of the contemporary world, it will have served its purpose. For the moment, however, it must begin with what is past: Vienna, capital of the Austro-Hungarian Empire, in the early 1860s.

1

Histories, 1856–84

'Biographical truth does not exist, and if it did we could not use it.'[1]

Let us begin at a particular historical moment in a particular place – the arrival of the four-year-old Sigismund Freud (he began signing his name 'Sigmund' only in his late teens) in Vienna in 1860, in the Jewish district of Leopoldstadt, accompanied by his younger sister Anna, his father, Jacob Freud (a trader in textiles), and his mother, Amalia. Despite his death in exile in Hampstead, London, on 23 September 1939, Freud will forever be associated with the city where he lived nearly all his life; a city that saw the birth of psychoanalysis as an idea in the 1890s, and some years later the formation of the movement that would eventually ensure his global fame and notoriety. Based on the publication of his greatest work, *The Interpretation of Dreams*, as the year turned from 1899 to 1900, it has been tempting to situate Freud in the context of fin-de-siècle Vienna, the 'city of dreams' as it is now often named, which witnessed an incredible artistic and intellectual flourishing – new forms of aesthetics, the reorganization of the tonal system in music, new graphic and decorative styles, and experiments in architectural design.

But to understand Freud's own cultural shaping, one needs to locate him within the earlier, broader historical context of the 1860s, when Vienna, as the administrative hub of the Habsburg Empire, was on the cusp of a process of modernization and

Michaelerplatz, Vienna, 1850–88.

liberalization after ten years of neo-absolutist rule. The fortunes of Middle European Jews in the nineteenth century depended on the ascendancy of political liberalism that, in Austria and its associated provinces, had remained weak compared with France or Britain, even after the revolutions of 1848. Following Austria's defeat in the Austro-Prussian war of 1866, which led to a new constitution for the dual monarchy of Austria-Hungary, the liberals were able to control certain areas of policy and further a programme of secularization, laissez-faire economics and the rolling back of certain State controls – at least for the more prosperous middle class. This dynamic moment of reform created opportunities in the imperial capital for Jews in particular, who, by 1867, had achieved material equality in law after centuries of marginalization, persecution, and political and economic restrictions. Not surprisingly, the later 1860s saw a peak in migration towards the capital, particularly from the Eastern provinces. Many of the Jews who would form part of Vienna's cultural elite by the turn of the century – including

Gustav Mahler, Victor Adler (founder of the Social Democratic Workers' Party) and the essayist Karl Kraus – were sons of Jewish merchants or industrialists from crownlands of the empire, Bohemia and Moravia (both now in the Czech Republic), or from Silesia (seized by Prussia in the 1700s).

Sigmund Freud's family were very much part of this westward move. Both his parents hailed from further east in Galicia – a province acquired by the Habsburgs with the partition of Poland at the end of the eighteenth century, now in western Ukraine. Born in Tysmenitz in 1815, Jacob Freud and his first wife, Sally Kanner, raised two sons – Sigmund's half-brothers, Emanuel (b. 1833) and Philipp (b. 1836) – while Jacob entered into a trading partnership with Sally's grandfather, through which the family established ties in Freiberg (now Příbor), a small town in Moravia. After Sally's death (*c.* 1852), it was here that Jacob brought Amalia Nathansohn, whom he married in 1855 (she was in fact his third wife, but little is known about the second, Rebecca), and Sigismund Freud was born on 6 May 1856. A younger brother, Julius, was born a year and a half later but died at eight months old. Of his time in Freiberg Freud retained very few memories, the most vivid being one he disguised in an episode attributed to an anonymous patient in his article 'Screen Memories' (1899): a steeply sloping meadow, dotted with dandelions, where he played with John and Pauline, the children of his half-brother Emanuel, while a Czech peasant woman and a nurse looked on. John, as we shall see, came to feature prominently in Freud's mental life. But for the time being, spurred by regional economic crises, the two halves of the family separated. Emanuel and Philipp emigrated to Manchester, England, in 1858, where they set up in business together importing goods from Germany and France, while Jacob and the rest of the family moved briefly to Leipzig, and then on to the imperial capital.

The attractions of Vienna were not only economic. They had to do with the temporary triumph of a liberal secularized ethos that

Freiberg (now Příbor), Moravia, *c.* 1845.

promised emancipation from the more controlled life of the ghetto. As the rabbi and political activist Joseph S. Bloch observed in 1885: 'To the Jew liberalism was more than just a political doctrine, a comfortable principle and a popular opinion of the day – it was his spiritual asylum . . . his patent of liberty after a slavery of indescribable severity and shame.'[2] Liberal culture was newly materialized in a series of grand building projects – the parliament, the town council, the university, the opera house – beginning in waves from 1861, which also saw the levelling of the medieval inner-city fortifications to create a circle of wide boulevards (similar to Baron Haussmann's mid-century transformation of Paris). Such works represented the displacement of aristocratic-federal and Catholic clerical power by an ascendant bourgeois class. Freud recalled his father bringing home portraits of the middle-class professionals who led the Bürgerministerium, the more confident liberal government of 1867, in order to adorn the house: 'henceforth every industrious Jewish schoolboy carried a Cabinet Minister's portfolio in his satchel.'[3]

Twinned with the liberal political project was a set of Enlightenment values, 'universal' and 'humanist', that stressed reason over religion, cosmopolitanism, the rights of individuals and a belief in the autonomy of the ethical will. These were associated specifically with a German Enlightenment tradition (not a local Austrian one) – that of Gotthold Ephraim Lessing, Immanuel Kant and Friedrich Schiller. Freud's Anglophilia, and his avid reading of Adam Smith, David Hume and J. S. Mill, has often been noted, but it is Schiller, Heinrich Heine and Johann Wolfgang von Goethe who loom most insistently as cultural reference points throughout his work. As Jewish scholar Gershom Scholem quipped: 'For many Jews the encounter with Friedrich Schiller was more real than their encounter with actual Germans.'[4] Freud repeatedly alludes to Schiller for confirmation of his view of hunger and love as the two basic drives of human psychology, and when he was awarded the Goethe Prize from the City of Frankfurt in 1930, he admitted that this late mark of recognition gave him a special pleasure.

The turn to liberalism among Habsburg Jews, then, brought with it an ideal of assimilation into a specifically German culture; German, adopted in the late eighteenth century as the official administrative language of the empire, was the symbol of a ruling elite in an increasingly polyglot society. It helps to remember that Germany itself, an unconsolidated empire until Bismarck's triumph in 1871, was at this point more of a linguistic and cultural ideal than a realized political entity. The price of such assimilation was often the abandonment of Judaic culture and religion: Arnold Schoenberg, Victor Adler and the psychoanalyst Alfred Adler all became Christian converts (notably to Protestantism, rather than Austrian Catholicism). But many of those who retained their Judaic identity in some form also still thought of themselves as culturally German. (Freud, for his part, claimed that his father had allowed him to grow up in complete ignorance of everything that concerned

Freud with his mother, Amalia, and younger sisters Rosa and Dolfi (Adolphine), *c.* 1864.

Judaism, although this seems to be an overstatement, as he received private tuition in Hebrew and later in life identified evermore strongly with his 'inner' Jewishness.)

The main institution through which the sons of middle-class Jews assimilated into Germanized high culture was the *Gymnasium*. This was a standard of elite secondary schools, akin to grammar schools, dedicated to Enlightenment humanist cultural development, which proved particularly attractive to Jewish families given the high value they traditionally placed on education (by around 1880, roughly a third of the *Gymnasium* students in Vienna were Jewish).[5] As the social historian Marsha Rozenblit notes, 'young men trained there surely knew more about Horace, Cicero, and the *Nibelungenlied* than they did about the Talmud and the Torah.'[6] Freud was at first schooled at home by his father, but in 1865 entered the *Realgymnasium* in Leopoldstadt, which had been founded a year earlier (it was renamed the

Sigmund-Freud-Gymnasium in 1989). By all accounts he fared exceptionally well here, earning a place at the top of his class. His sister Anna recalls his absorption in learning throughout his teens, when he would take his meals alone in his room in order not to be distracted from his studies (the family was not well off, and out of the seven children – five younger sisters, and his younger brother, Alexander – Sigmund was the only one to have his own bedroom).[7] During this time he gained the thorough grounding in Latin, Greek and classical civilization reflected in his later fascination with archaeology, famously memorialized in his naming of the 'Oedipus complex'.

There is, then, something typical about Freud's early life – even down to his prevarication over a career in law or medicine when he graduated *summa cum laude* at the age of seventeen. At any rate, it was as a medical student that he enrolled in the University of Vienna in the autumn of 1873, then one of the pre-eminent centres for medical research in the world. The degree allowed for a broad scientific curriculum, taught in the philosophy faculty: anatomy, physiology and biology, but also Darwinism, magnetism, electricity, chemistry and mathematics, which Freud supplemented by taking courses in philosophy and logic with the Catholic philosopher Franz Brentano. University medicine did not necessarily funnel one towards a career as a doctor; it equally opened up the realm of natural scientific research, which, in Vienna in the 1870s, was dominated by the influence of a positivist, mechanist orientation towards the study of life formulated by Emil du Bois-Reymond and Ernst von Brücke in Berlin in the 1840s. These two friends, joined by Hermann von Helmholtz in 1845, famously swore 'to assert the truth that no forces operate in the organism other than those common to physics and chemistry'.[8] Du Bois-Reymond's key work of 1848 explored the relationship between muscle tissue and electricity in animals, and in the same year Helmholtz published his famous treatise on the conservation of energy, moving on to study the physiology of perception. Brücke moved to Vienna in 1849, the first of many foreign appointments designed to modernize the faculty, and founded a research institute for the investigation of physiology, bringing the positivist programme with him.

If Freud appeared to vacillate between nature and medicine throughout his studies – in 1875 he wrote to his close friend from school, Eduard Silberstein, of his decision to take his PhD in philosophy and zoology, but then returned from a visit to his half-brother's family in Manchester impressed by advances in contemporary medicine – it is clear that medicine, for him, meant mostly natural scientific research. In this respect he planned to go to Berlin to benefit from the lectures of du Bois-Reymond and Helmholtz in the winter of 1874, but this fell through, presumably owing to lack of funds. However, in the spring of 1876 he began his career as a researcher while still pursuing his undergraduate studies, and was chosen by the zoologist Carl Claus to undertake a study at his new institute for marine biology in Trieste (then part of the Adriatic possessions of the Habsburg Empire). The project was anatomical dissection in search of the sexual organs of eels: '6.30 in the evening, hands stained with the white and red blood of marine animals, cell detritus swimming before my eyes, which disturbs me even in my dreams, in my thoughts nothing but the great problems connected with the words ducts, testicles, and ovaries,' Freud wrote jokingly to Silberstein.[9] In the same year Freud joined Brücke's institute, where he pursued further research until 1882 (having completed his medical degree in 1881).

Besides the draw of cutting-edge scientific discovery, Freud was attracted by the positivist approach itself, which again had associations with a German culture of liberalism, progress and modernity. Claus and Brücke were both German (as indeed would be other figures crucial in Freud's training, such as the university's Chair of Psychiatry, Theodor Meynert, and humanist professor

Freud family portrait, Vienna, 1878. Back row, left to right: Paula, Anna, Sigmund, Emanuel (half-brother), Rosa, Marie, Simon Nathanson. Front row: Dolfi, ?, Amalia, Alexander, ?, Jacob.

of medicine Hermann Nothnagel). Claus was a key mediator of Darwinist ideas on the continent, and Brücke was known for his anti-clerical sympathies. Freud's letters from this period enthuse about the radical materialist philosophy of Ludwig Feuerbach, and he described himself to Silberstein in 1875 as a 'godless medical man and empiricist'.[10]

At the heart of Freud's research interests lay the fields of neuroanatomy and neurophysiology. Questions concerning the exact function of nerves – conceived on the foundation of basic physical or mechanical forces and tracked down with the aid of dissection, microscopy and electrical apparatuses – link together the, at first glance, curious range of topics in his papers, from his first anatomical publications on nerve roots in the spinal cord of the fish *Ammocoetes* (*Petromyzon planeri*) (1877) and the nerve fibres in freshwater crayfish (1882), to articles on new

histological procedures for staining nerve tracts (as a preparation
for microscopic study), and his series of papers on the effects
and medical uses of cocaine (1884). Though Freud has been
credited with 'nearly' discovering the anaesthetic properties of
cocaine (a lead mentioned in one of his papers was acted on by
the ophthalmologist Carl Koller), his focus in these latter papers
was more on the physiological effects of the alkaloid on mood
and muscular power. A similar focus on biophysical functioning
is reflected in the work of his older colleagues in the institute,

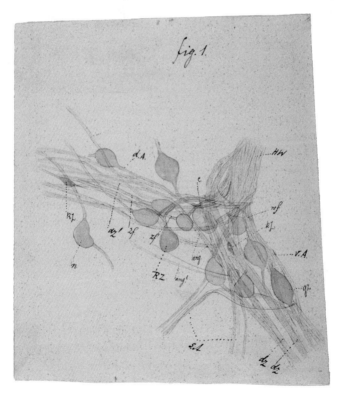

Freud's original drawing of the spinal ganglia of the lamprey *Petromyzon planeri* (now
Lampetra planeri), 1878.

Sigmund Exner, Ernst Fleischl von Marxow and Josef Breuer, the latter two of whom would become close friends. Von Marxow published on the law of nerve excitation, and Exner attempted a physiological explanation of psychic phenomena (as would Freud himself in the mid-1890s). Breuer turned to nervous diseases, and would become Freud's senior collaborator on *Studies in Hysteria* (1895), discussed in the next chapter, but his previous publications ranged across topics such as respiratory regulation and the function of otoliths in the ear (involving a collaboration with the Viennese philosopher and physicist Ernst Mach). It was in this dynamic research environment that Freud spent his happiest hours at the university.

With all these side projects going on, it took Freud eight years to complete his medical degree – a fact he would later put down to youthful dilatoriness. But Freud was evidently no idler, and the long period spent at the Institute of Physiology had just as much to do with his struggle to find an optimal opening in the research field: close enough to natural science to satisfy his intellectual bent, but practical enough to sustain him financially. A key factor here was Freud's engagement in June 1882 to Martha Bernays, the daughter of a linen merchant from Hamburg and sister of Eli Bernays, who in the same period was courting Freud's sister Anna (they later emigrated to America where their son, Edward Bernays, was instrumental in founding the field of public relations). Freud and Martha first met in April 1882, only two months later making a secret agreement to be married when circumstances permitted. He immediately resigned his position at the laboratory – partly under Brücke's advice, given that there was no immediate chance of gaining an assistant position at the institute. He now sought to gain as much clinical experience as possible in a short space of time at the General Hospital of Vienna – experience that would be necessary for setting up in private practice. After a brief stint in surgery, he worked under Hermann Nothnagel as an *Aspirant*

Martha Bernays, 1880.

(clinical assistant, the lowliest position in internal medicine), then for six months as *Sekundararzt* (junior physician) in Theodor Meynert's psychiatric clinic, in the summer of 1883, followed by dermatology and ophthalmology, receiving his title of *Dozent* (lecturer) in neuropathology in 1885. Although unsalaried, this title, in principle, allowed him to lecture at the university, and thus establish a reputation that would attract better-paying patients.

Clinically Freud's eye was still on research rather than therapeutic accomplishments, but this reflects the ethos at the Vienna medical school, famous for its association with 'therapeutic nihilism'. The object was not so much to cure as to turn pathological anatomy into a diagnostic tool, correlating the visible signs of illness in the living with discoveries on the autopsy table, an approach pioneered by the renowned pathologist Carl Rokitansky in the late 1830s. This seeming indifference to human life also explains the receptivity of the medical faculty (including Meynert, who provided Freud with a space to continue his neurological investigations in the Institute of Cerebral Anatomy) to Arthur Schopenhauer's pessimistic philosophy of the human will. There is a nice vignette of Freud describing his absorbed attendance on a dying patient to his fiancée, Martha Bernays, in 1884, which in fact led to his first clinical publication ('A Case of Cerebral Haemorrhage'). Freud had found a number of symptoms from which to deduce the locality of the patient's haemorrhage, so sat beside him all afternoon observing the 'variable development of the illness till seven o'clock, when symmetrical paralysis appeared, with the result that until his death at 8 p.m. nothing escaped my notice'. The publication of the case was 'imperative', especially should the autopsy yield a satisfactory confirmation of the diagnosis.[11] Freud's bedside manner can hardly have brought much comfort to the patient.

There was a further factor affecting Freud's shift from academic life to medical practice, however: the changing political atmosphere in Vienna, which by the later 1870s had turned against both the liberals and the Jews. Though the liberal ministry of 1867 must have seemed to the schoolboy Freud like a vindication of the eternal voice of reason and progress, during his student years the political and economic map of Europe was being redrawn in ways that would have catastrophic consequences for Germanized Jews and the liberal regime on which their wager of assimilation depended. The Habsburg defeat by Bismarck's forces in the Austro-Prussian war, which in the short term bolstered the liberal position – Freud's sister Anna recalls how affected Sigmund was by seeing the wounded arrive at Vienna's North Station, and how he urged the family to make 'charpie', linen thread for surgical dressing – had also resulted in an emergent German empire from which Austria was excluded. This left those German-leaning subjects of the Habsburg Empire outside the nation with which they might have politically and culturally identified.

At the same time, the structure of Franz Joseph's unwieldy conglomerate of kingdoms, crownlands and provinces was coming under increased pressure from other nascent national movements (the same defeat had led to Hungarian home rule, but Czech nationalism and Serbian nationalism were also on the rise). It is in the light of this incipient collapse that Theodor Herzl (another Jewish immigrant to Vienna, but from Hungarian Pest, in 1878) would eventually develop his Zionist vision for a Jewish homeland in Palestine. There was a period during the 1870s and early 1880s when a younger generation of Viennese Jews, such as Herzl, Victor Adler, Gustav Mahler, the writer Arthur Schnitzler and even Freud himself, would become entangled in German cultural nationalism (Freud was briefly a member of the *Leseverein der deutschen Studenten Wien*, or German Students Reading Club, at university in the mid-1870s). Hence the terrible irony when in 1885 the Austrian activist for the Pan-German movement Georg Schönerer added a clause to its manifesto calling for the 'removal of Jewish influence from all sections of public life'.[12]

The earliest recollection of antisemitism that Freud shares in his autobiographical statements is a conversation had when out for a walk with his father sometime around 1867 (though the incident related occurred just prior to Jacob's marriage in 1851). Keen to emphasize how much better things were in the emerging liberal period, Jacob recounted:

When I was a young man . . . I went for a walk one
Saturday in the streets of your birthplace [Freiberg];
I was well dressed, and had a new fur cap on my head.

A Christian came up to me and with a single blow knocked off my cap into the mud and shouted: Jew! get off the pavement!' 'And what did you do?' I asked. 'I went into the roadway and picked up my cap,' was his quiet reply.[13]

As we will see later, the conversation, and his father's inability to stand up to his oppressor, had a profound effect on Freud's imaginative life. Nevertheless, when Freud enrolled in the University of Vienna in 1873 – which coincided with the crash of the Vienna Stock Exchange that unleashed a wave of antisemitic hatred – Freud found that he too 'was expected to feel myself inferior and an alien because I was a Jew'.[14] He 'refused absolutely to do the first of these things'; but this implies the second was unavoidable. As Schnitzler, who also studied medicine at the university in the early 1880s, recalled: 'It was impossible, especially for a Jew in the public eye, to ignore the fact that he was a Jew, for the others did not . . . One had the choice of being regarded as insensitive, pushy and arrogant, or hypersensitive, shy and paranoid.'[15]

In 1883 Freud recorded a more direct brush with antisemitic feeling, when on a train journey through Saxony he upset his fellow travellers by opening the window. 'There came a shout from the background: "He's a dirty Jew!"', and there was almost a brawl, though Freud, it seems, managed to face off the challenge by standing his ground. Still the incident captures the insecurity and latent threat Freud must have been aware of on a daily basis. Liberal influence was now in decline, a key factor being the extension of suffrage in 1882, which fuelled the rise of more populist politics and the eventual triumph of the Christian Social Party and their antisemitic leader, Karl Lueger, in 1895. Indeed, it was liberalism's identification with Jews that hastened its collapse.

Freud's letters of the early 1880s are full of reflections on the 'struggle for existence'. We have a lot of insight into his situation during this period because of his almost daily correspondence

Antisemitic cartoon published shortly after the Viennese stock market crash, in *Kikeriki*, 18 May 1873.

with Martha Bernays, who had accompanied her mother to live in Wandsbek, just outside Hamburg, in June 1883. Even though Martha pressed him not to abandon his intellectual goals for her sake, Freud was keenly aware that the temptation to devote his life to scientific research might 'destroy our chances of sharing a life': 'I have worked long enough for nothing.'[16] The years between 1881 and 1885 were financially and emotionally tortuous. Neurophysiologist that he was, he worried that the struggle to keep all his options open would endanger his own nervous system, but he managed to keep things going with the support of colleagues such as Breuer and Josef Paneth (his replacement in Brücke's laboratory), both of whom loaned him money: 'We are all poor and promise to help one another whenever we can.'[17]

On the face of it, the 'struggle' was about economic competition and the scarcity of university appointments. Advancement at the University of Vienna depended, in principle, on clinical publications, but these required access to a stream of useful cases through the university's clinical departments. Yet Breuer's excellent reputation as a sought-after physician in private practice was ironically an obstacle to Freud's own advancement. Nothnagel suggested that Freud set up in a provincial town, with the aim of returning to Vienna when Breuer retired. Still, a significant factor affecting the choices open to Freud was undoubtedly prejudice against Jews – even if, later on, from a position of financial security and international recognition, he would present this as formative of his strength of mind: 'I put up, without much regret, with my non-acceptance into the community'; being 'made familiar with the fate of being in Opposition' laid the foundations 'for a certain degree of independence of judgment'.[18] Nevertheless, several of Freud's dreams analysed within *The Interpretation of Dreams* deal with rivalries among colleagues, all of whom are competing hopefully for promotions that never arrive due to 'denominational' factors. 'None of you realizes how badly people such as ourselves are affected by these matters,' Breuer complained uncharacteristically in a letter to Adolf Exner in 1894. In the same year, only two out of 53 Jews teaching at the university reached the highest positions.[19]

There was, then, more than economic uncertainty affecting Freud's gradual, hesitant disengagement from the academy. His letters are full of a poignant sense of loss, frustration and anxiety. At the same time, however, his commitment to Martha, and therefore to making himself financially independent, gave him a specific goal, and a point of existential and emotional anchorage. Bit by bit, as their relationship gained in trust through the protracted exchange of letters, Freud gradually achieved his first footholds in professional life. He never wholly discarded his commitment to research, but gradually made it an offshoot of his working practice as a physician. The end of 1884 saw a turning point in his self-confidence. By now he had a string of scientific publications, including his first clinical articles on neuropathology; he had published the first of a series of papers on the physiological effects of cocaine; he felt close to attaining his *Dozentur* (submitted in January, and ratified in September 1885); he had gained direct clinical experience and was getting bits of salaried work in the hospital, and was therefore almost ready to set up in independent practice – therefore confident, too, that he might soon be united with Martha: 'it will mean the end of the sponger's existence and the beginning of the end of the "*Dalles*" [Yiddish, meaning "poverty"],' he wrote to her in November 1884.[20] Though another ten years would pass before Freud achieved his scientific breakthrough and formulated the basis of psychoanalysis, the 28-year-old had seemingly completed his intellectual and professional formation and was on the cusp of setting up as a practising neurologist.

The Other Life: An Alternative History

What does this brief history leave out? From the point of view of the theories for which Freud would eventually become famous: almost everything. Freud's mature work would leave wholly changed the sense of what a history of the self could be, how memories interconnect and relate to external experiences, or what strings a life together. For instance, his most significant discovery – still in the future at this point – would concern the fundamentally dual nature of personal life. On the face of it, there are the memories, facts and narratives that we consciously recall about ourselves, of the kind that I have outlined in the first half of this chapter. But there is also an alternate history, composed of *unconscious* memories and fantasies, of which we can at most catch glimpses in our dreams, or in the irrational worries and anxieties that plague our attempts to achieve an unruffled, stable knowledge of ourselves and our environment. What does it mean to set out the narrative of Freud's early life – to 'make sense' of it and put it into sequence – without attending to these, for him, compelling alternative dimensions?

To give an example: Freud's verdict on his experiences of antisemitism in his more public autobiographical pronouncements tends to be terse, defiant, unsentimental. But later on, in his free associations to his own dreams (made public in *The Interpretation of Dreams*), he would reveal a far more complex, affect-laden set of responses. In one of many dreams featuring the city of Rome, he is forced to flee from the city with his children and finds himself sitting on the edge of a fountain, 'greatly depressed and almost in tears'.[21] The dream was in part prompted by Freud's seeing Theodor Herzl's play *The New Ghetto* (1898), which dealt with 'the Jewish problem' and 'concern about the future of one's children, to whom one cannot give a country of their own'.[22] Shortly before that dream he had heard that another Jew had been 'obliged to resign the position which he had painfully achieved in the State asylum'.[23] A further Rome dream prompts Freud to recall his sympathy with the Carthaginians, rather than Romans, while studying the Punic Wars in his school years – this was the time that he 'began to understand for the first time what it meant to belong to an alien race'.[24] It is this dream that then leads him to recognize the long-range effects of the conversation with his father about the antisemitic attack in the street, after which Freud had (in his mind) contrasted his father's response with that of Hannibal's father, who had made his son swear vengeance on Rome: 'Ever since that time Hannibal had had a place in my phantasies.'[25]

Such incidents, emerging out of Freud's documentation of his dream life, resonate trans-historically in ways that complicate the relation of past to present, real to unreal, one person's experience to another's. They complicate the task of telling a life. Professional disappointments, antisemitic prejudice, Freud's classical education and that of his children, are unconsciously interwoven in Freud's mental life with the historic exile of the Jews (Freud's sorrow at the fountain in the dream recalls the biblical psalm 'By the waters of Babylon'). His dreams also frequently manifest the desire to traverse symbolic boundaries between different identities and different languages. In the dream that links to thoughts of Hannibal, Freud was surprised to find so many posters in German. A day earlier, while discussing a place to meet with a friend from Berlin, he had warned that Prague might not be so hospitable for a German, and had secretly wished the meeting could take place in Rome; in the dream in which Freud is fleeing Rome, his son pronounces a secret word, a Hebrew neologism – *Ungeseres* – the opposite of *Geseres*, or 'imposed doom'. Experience is here rendered ambiguous and polyvocal, like the image of Rome itself: cherished seat of classical culture, and beloved of Goethe, but also source of a conflict between Roman Catholicism and Judaism, and in classical times the city that Hannibal turned back from in his Italian campaign, leading to the subsequent retaliation and destruction of Carthage.

Though consideration of such deeply layered and personal material involves stepping out of chronological sequence, drawing on associations that emerged from Freud's self-analysis and work on dreams in the later 1890s, it is useful to include some of these details now, as they engage with his youth and student years from an entirely different angle. Equally pertinent are the fundamental questions that *The Interpretation of Dreams* poses as to what a life is, and how we should understand or represent it. Freud's approach to mental life, as we shall see, is in many ways 'historical'. But it is a history whose narrative, as in the Rome examples just given, is integrated according to rather different principles – psychological and even somatic – from conventional accounts. It begins by not taking memory at face value; or, rather, by revealing aspects of memory that have the power to dissolve our conventional grip on reality, to disturb our more settled narratives with the revelation of another life, more secret, more disturbing.

At first sight the early memories that Freud began to reveal in *The Interpretation of Dreams* and allied works seem banal, even trivial. One is the scene already mentioned, of Freud in the meadow in Freiberg playing with his niece and nephew when he was perhaps three years old. Another, one of his earliest memories from Vienna, is of tearing up an album with coloured plates that illustrated a journey through Persia, together with his sister Anna; a third is of being reprimanded by his father after 'obeying the call of nature' in front of his parents in their bedroom. Perhaps these last two might count as childish indiscretions, of the kind that add colour to many such autobiographies – for instance Jean-Jacques Rousseau being beaten by his nurse, or Goethe's earliest memory of throwing the family crockery out of the window.

However, the key lies not so much in the remembered scenes themselves as in the link they provide to unconscious processes of thinking: the underbelly of our mental life. Freud was not the first to argue that our 'conscious' life must have an 'unconscious' dimension behind it – the thoughts and ideas we are able to recall and articulate being but the end result of more extensive, hidden and automatic processes, triggered by latent neurological, mnemic and somatic systems. Such notions of a mental unconscious were still very much contested, particularly by those scientists, moralists, philosophers or theologians who, for many different reasons, sought to uphold a paradigm of consciousness as an autonomous logical or psychological entity. As Franz Brentano observed in his *Psychology from an Empirical Standpoint*, published in 1874, around the time Freud was attending his lectures, 'to postulate an unconscious consciousness' would seem absurd to many people; John Stuart Mill considered it a 'direct contradiction'.[26] Still, those committed to a post-Darwinist, materialist account of human phenomena were, as a matter of course, beginning to try to theorize the relation of thought to a murkier somatic and affective hinterland. In the same work Brentano cites the English physician Henry Maudsley's attempt to ground consciousness on physiological description, as well as experimental psychologist Wilhelm Wundt's belief that the mind could make unconscious inferences, and philosopher and 'psycho-physicist' Gustav Fechner's suggestion that ideas and sensations need to reach a certain threshold of intensity before they become conscious.[27]

What made Freud's stance different (though akin to Schopenhauer's and Nietzsche's) was his claim that the unconscious logic determining our access to consciousness by no means mirrors the portrait of the mind we like to present, as a rational, reflective apparatus with which we manage accounts of the world and our relations to others. For instance, one destabilizing element Freud introduces into his account of recollection is falsification. Reflecting on the origins of his own earliest memories, he ascertains that some, at least, are retrospective constructions based on scenes that his parents had repeatedly described to him.[28] Others, such as the luminous meadow in Freiberg – Freud's only 'plastic' impression of his place of birth – give rise to the suspicion that they are composites in which elements of an original childhood experience have been displaced by impressions of a later date, grafted together to form what Freud calls a 'screen memory'. The 'screen', or 'covering over', refers to a tendency to disguise or replace disagreeable impressions with more pleasant ones. Freud suggests that not only the presentation of the remembered scene, but its very selection – the seemingly tame scene over a more dramatic one – may have nothing to do with historical accuracy. Indeed, it may be questioned 'whether we have any memories at all *from* our childhood'.[29] What we have instead are memories *relating* to childhood, designed as much to bury the past as to reveal it.

Another feature that challenges our familiarity with the narrative of any life – our own included – is, ironically, the 'hypermnesic' quality of memory itself. The degree to which our unconscious minds are able to retain tiny, seemingly insignificant details from our past far outweighs the few impressions we habitually have at our disposal. During the 1890s Freud would dream about a one-eyed doctor, who it turns out really did feature in the earliest years of his childhood: 'It was thirty-eight years since I had seen the doctor, and so far as I know I had never thought of him in my waking life.'[30] He gives similar examples from other people's dreams – a young man dreams of a lion, which he later recognizes as a china object, once his 'favourite toy during his early childhood'.[31] The Belgian psychologist Joseph Delboeuf had a dream about a procession of lizards in 1862; in 1877, looking through an old periodical, he refound the illustration that, in the distant past, must have been the origin of the dream image.[32] According to Delboeuf, 'even the most insignificant impression leaves an unalterable trace, which is indefinitely capable of revival.'[33]

However, if the past is indefinitely capable of revival, then does it not also lose the quality of being past? Freud's nephew John, for instance, who plays with him in the possibly falsified meadow scene in Freiberg, was his earliest model of a playmate: 'Until the end of my third year we had been inseparable. We had loved each other and fought with each other.'[34] John never entirely outgrows those impressions in Freud's mind. When he comes to visit from England in his teenage years, it is as a 'revenant' of that earliest relationship. More than this, John 'had a determining influence on all my subsequent relations with contemporaries'.[35] All of Freud's friends – so he comes to understand – have been re-incarnations of this first figure, like ghosts in the underworld that, in a favourite analogy of Freud's drawn from Homer's *Odyssey*, 'awoke to new life as soon as they tasted blood'.[36]

So far, so uncanny: on the one hand, according to Freud, our actual recollections are possibly falsifications; on the other, we contain a vast reservoir of impressions, only a tiny portion of which we consciously have access to, and this concealed past has the power to repeat itself indefinitely. But there are further twists to Freud's account of memory. First, the past's power to return and infect the experience of the present gives special force to our earliest experiences – to our life as a child. This is particularly clear during the night, when our conscious management of thought switches off to a certain extent. As Freud would comment at the end of the 1890s: 'to our surprise, we find the child and the child's impulses still living on in the dream.'[37] At the very least, this complicates our understanding of biographical progression: in the Freudian life, one only apparently leaves the child behind.

But there is more to this. The mental life of the child operates along different lines from the adult: 'Children are completely egoistic; they feel their needs intensely and strive ruthlessly to satisfy them – especially as against the rivals, other children, and first and foremost as against their brothers and sisters.'[38] Freud becomes interested in the way children, who may grow up to be supremely ethical beings, feel no compunction in tearing the wings off beetles and butterflies, and give free rein to instinctual impulses. More strongly than this, he believed that adults who love their brothers and sisters, and would feel bereaved at their death, may at the same time 'harbour evil wishes against them in their unconscious, dating from earlier times'.[39] 'I wish Josefine was dead,' a child commented to her father. "Why dead?" enquired her father soothingly, "wouldn't it do if she went away?" "No," replied the child; "then she'd come back again."'[40] Freud supposed that he himself had welcomed the death of his baby brother Julius with 'adverse wishes and genuine childish jealousy'.[41] Thus not only do we lose trust in our sense of memory, but the aspects of our mind concealed behind it are morally untrustworthy because they are infantile, perhaps even dangerous. This dangerous child accompanies us in the shadows.

Freud thinks of these unconscious layers of recollection, in which our acquired morality and rationality is subverted by a more infantile and instinctually driven past, in somatic terms. Dreams can often reflect obvious bodily urges, such as the desire to urinate, or to drink. In *The Interpretation of Dreams* he recounts how the explorer Mungo Park, 'when he was almost dying of thirst on one of his African journeys, dreamt unceasingly of the well-watered valleys and meadows of his home'.[42] And of course, Freud is famous for the central weight he gives to sexuality, and the domination of aspects of our thought by displaced erotic wishes and libidinal impulses. But there are moments in which Freud – by training deeply embedded in physiological approaches – represents thinking itself as a layered system for either discharging or inhibiting quantities of excitation. We are aware of the way a joke not only delights the mind but can provoke a nervous release that shakes the whole body with laughter. But what if all kinds of cognitive acts – including not only joking or dreaming, but remembering – play a functional role at the behest of our bodies, acting sometimes as a safety valve that protects us from troubling feelings and tensions. We create stories that both our minds and our bodies are able to live with. Hence Freud's mischievous statement placed at the head of this chapter: 'biographical truth is not to be had, and even if one had it, one could not use it.'

There is a final piece of the puzzle I want to introduce here, in advance, from Freud's work of the 1890s – his theory of 'repression' and censorship. The unconscious may well be a vast repository of undying memories and instinctual wishes, but everyone has wishes 'that he would prefer not to disclose to other people, and wishes that he will not admit even to himself'.[43] Therefore, between the unconscious and consciousness lies a system designed to inhibit the appearance of unwanted thoughts or desires, which allows nothing to pass unmodified, especially if it might provoke internal conflicts, anxieties or unpleasure. In a striking image, Freud compared the doctored scenes to which consciousness more routinely has access with 'the peace that has descended upon a battlefield strewn with corpses; no trace is left of the struggle which raged over it'.[44] Like the meadow in Freiberg – 'green and thickly grown . . . We are picking the yellow flowers' – what trace is left here of the frequent bouts of aggression that, from family sources, Freud knew were an essential part of the dynamic of his childhood play with his nephew?

I have now listed several ways in which Freud, in his mature work, began to rethink the function of memory and consiousness – not only in anticipation of the chapters ahead, but as a prelude to considering his early development from an entirely different, more psychoanalytic perspective. Alone, however, none of the features of mental life I've outlined quite captures the nature of the 'hidden life' I am trying to evoke, in which the very model of the liberal subject, with its belief in history as progress, and its subservience to principles of truth, self-consciousness and rational motivation, is potentially overturned. In the narrative outlined in the first half of the chapter, the youthful Freud is driven by humanist, liberal, scientific ideals. In the counter-narrative Freud will evolve, the life-history of the person is differently centred: an abundance of unconscious trains of thought radiates secretly outwards from certain repressed or forgotten childhood experiences, and therefore consigns us to not really knowing who we are, or the reasons why we act. In the unconscious we encounter a complete 'transvaluation of all psychical values' (Freud borrows the phrase from Nietzsche).[45] To give a sense of what this actually means in practice, I will introduce a dream of Freud's – not, at this point, to explain his theory of how dreams work, but simply to give an example of how all the impressions of his early life, and the layers of his own history, become reorganized and 'transvalued' in such a telling. They reveal a different kind of person, a different biography, even a different sense of time. The dream is known as Freud's dream of 'Count Thun'.

Freud most likely dreamed this dream in the early hours of the morning, at some point in August 1898, while travelling alone in a train compartment – without a lavatory – en route to his vacation in Bad Aussee in the Austrian state of Styria. There are a few useful details he adds about the evening preceding the dream. While waiting in the Westbahnhof railway station in Vienna, Freud had been struck by the sight of Count Thun, former Governor of Bohemia and current Prime Minister of the Interior, pushing arrogantly past a ticket inspector 'with a curt motion of his hand'. Freud then spent the rest of his time on the station platform keeping his eyes open lest anyone lay claim to a reserved compartment by pulling rank. Having paid the full first-class fare himself, he intended in this case to 'make a loud protest: that is to say to claim equal rights'.[46] He then gives an account of his dream (one of the longest in *The Interpretation of Dreams*) from which I'll

Wilhelm Wörnle, after Siegmund L'Allemand, engraving of Count Franz Anton von Thun and Hohenstein, 1893.

reproduce a few sections to give a sense of the way Freud conveys its seemingly random, inconsequential content:

A crowd of people, a meeting of students. – A count (Thun or Taaffe) was speaking. He was challenged to say something about the Germans, and declared with a contemptuous gesture that their favourite flower was colt's foot, and put some sort of dilapidated leaf – or rather the crumpled skeleton of a leaf – into his buttonhole . . .

(Then, less distinctly:) It was as though I was in the Aula [the ceremonial hall of the University of Vienna]*; the entrances were cordoned off and we had to escape, I made my way through a series of beautifully furnished rooms, evidently ministerial or public apartments, with furniture upholstered in a colour between brown and violet . . .*

Once more I was in front of the station, but this time in the company of an elderly gentleman. I thought of a plan for remaining unrecognized; and then saw that this plan had already been put into effect. It was as though thinking and experiencing were one and the same thing. He appeared to be blind, at all events with one eye, and I handed him a male glass urinal (which we had to buy or had bought in town). So I was a sick-nurse and had to give him the urinal because he was blind. If the ticket-collector were to see us like that, he would be certain to let us get away without noticing us. Here the man's attitude and his micturating penis appeared in plastic form. (This was the point at which I awoke, feeling a need to micturate.)

That, at least, is the surface report of the dream, what Freud will call the 'manifest' content. But there follows about twelve more pages of description I can only loosely summarize here, which attempt to tease out the myriad threads of thought running through his mind that day, of which – according to the theory

– the dream is the condensed product. The method Freud uses to restore the wider mental context of the dream is that of free association – taking each single detail separately and seeing what links or recollections it calls to mind in an effort to re-traverse, as spontaneously as possible, the route that brought precisely these fragments and scenes into the same dream on the same night. It is this 'latent content', revealed by the analysis and bursting at the seams with a multitude of voices, characters and episodes, which affords numerous alternative insights into Freud's life and upbringing – essentially, what it was like to 'be' Freud.

Freud's reconstruction is compressed, but also riotous and fascinating (the full account can be found in *The Interpretation of Dreams*). Freud pursues his mental associations across six different languages – German, Italian (he recalls humming Figaro's aria on the station platform), French, English (scenes from Shakespeare's *Henry vi*), Spanish and Latin. As this broader mental map unfolds, it covers several provinces and countries (Styria, Moravia, Saxony, England) and engages distinct historical layers from every decade of Freud's life. There are the immediate circumstances of 1898 (including references to the upcoming Golden Jubilee of the Habsburg emperor), and – taking off from the ailing gentleman at the end of the dream – connections to the final stages of his father's illness and death two years previously.

Other threads link to a large number of the events and themes already covered in our more 'overt' history of Freud's youth: for instance, one strand of associations, to do with flowers, leads to red and white carnations, the former a symbol of the Social Democrats, the latter of the antisemitic Christian Social Party; the student meeting at the opening of the dream recalls to Freud his involvement in German nationalism through the radical German Students Reading Club in his early university years; the same moment triggers a memory of a conspiracy he led against an unpopular master at the *Gymnasium*.

Finally, the dream analysis leads Freud to recollect the scene, when he was seven or eight, of relieving himself in his parents' bedroom, which prompted his father's admonition: 'The boy will come to nothing.' Behind this lies an even older episode from when Freud was two, known to him only through hearsay, in which he wet the bed but consoled his father by promising to buy him a new one. Apart from various other historical markers – references to the revolutions of 1848, and the Plantagenets – the dream associations also provide an intriguing microcosm of Freud's perception of class hierarchies, as he weaves his way through a Kafkaesque (another Habsburg German-Jewish writer) world of railway officials, government councillors, imperious aristocrats, lurking housekeepers, coachmen and prostitutes.

It is palpably Freud's life – but sequenced and interconnected according to a very different and disreputable logic than the history recounted earlier. What do we learn about Freud via this alternative mode of autobiography, condensed into a single night's dream? How does it recast our sense of Freud's development? For a start, there is no sense of development here. Even though the dream is full of references to actual events, none of these are historically interconnected: they are not ordered according to any sense of the passage of time. Rather, they are associated often through quite rogue elements, linked by a particular sound, or word. To take one example: the flower, 'colt's foot' (*Huflattich*), supposedly a favourite of the Germans, which the count refers to dismissively at the start of the dream, reminds Freud of the French *pisse-en-lit* (dandelion, but literally 'pissing in bed'), which takes him to the childhood bed-wetting incident. The French term also recalls Émile Zola's *La Terre* (1887), in which there is a farting competition – *flatus* (linking back to *-flattich*) – which Freud then associates with the inscription on the medal struck to commemorate the English victory over the Spanish Armada – *Flavit et dissipate sunt* (He blew and they were scattered).[47] Given the multiplicity of associations Freud makes as he attempts to reconstruct the thoughts and impulses behind the dream, it becomes easy to see why the interpretation is so much more voluminous – more crazy, even – than the dream itself.

What these associations are mapping is not historical or geographic relations, but a kind of neurological kinship. They are psychologically connected in Freud's mind – possibly even at the level of nerve fibres and neurones, but certainly as 'chains of association'. Memories of past and present, though separated in time, become mentally contiguous here – co-existing and compressed into a surreal limbo without borders or conventional narrative logic, in which a whole string of characters and situations are inappropriately, absurdly, overlaid by one another. For this reason it is hard to reduce a dream to a single message, or a single outcome. Rather than reading scenes sequentially, Freud encourages us to look for concentrations of meaning, points at which numerous layers appear to intersect.

If two of the overt triggers for the dream are, first, Freud's affront at (perhaps also fascination with) the arrogance of Count Thun, and, second, the need to urinate that finally wakes him, then a submerged nodal point between the two is the memory of his childish enjoyment at urinating in his parents' room, and the consequent rebuke from his father. It is the suppressed anger at this humiliation – and perhaps the remembered joy of the physical relief and excitement of exhibitionism – which appears to resonate across all the other layers of mental association, at least on this night: the antisemitic confrontation on the train to Saxony; a quarrel from his student years; even the Wars of the Roses. The implication here is that, just as Freud's nephew John becomes a 'revenant', so the childhood peeing incident never goes away: references to this scene constantly recur in Freud's dreams, and they do so in a way that is 'always linked with an enumeration of my achievements and successes', as if to counter his father's judgement that he will come to nothing.[48] If the dream has any logic, then – as far as

Freud is concerned – it is one that wishfully desires to overturn all these other situations of humiliation, culminating in the revenge that the dream takes on his own father by reversing their roles in the childhood scene: 'The older man (clearly my father, since his blindness in one eye referred to his unilateral glaucoma) was now micturating in front of me, just as I had in front of him.'[49]

This dream has justly attracted attention, particularly from biographers wanting to find in it some clue as to Freud's relationship with politics. The cultural historian Carl E. Schorske read it as a displacement of Freud's frustration with professional and social obstructions in the outer world – his lack of economic means, his marginalization and the antisemitic prejudices – into a conflict of the inner world. Here Count Thun, and countless other rivals and functionaries, could be vanquished by being symbolically identified with an inner struggle in which Freud is more able to emerge the victor: 'The "political" problem was dissolved in the final scene on the platform, where the dream work substituted the dying father for the living count.' The suggestion is that this is a flight from political engagement – albeit towards scientific achievements – which informs Freud's whole mature turn to psychological work.[50]

No doubt aspects of this reading are true. Freud himself recognized the ways in which dreams, thoroughly egoistic as they are in his view, compensate for shortcomings in real life by defensively rearranging the truth, always to the credit of the dreamer. However, to infer that this might apply to the framework of Freud's dream project itself – to taint it with a sense of 'escape' from reality – seems a mistake. That criticism would only stand if everything Freud materializes in his theory of unconscious associations – from the longevity of memories and their affect-laden qualities to the formative nature of infantile life – was untrue, an illusion. But this is tantamount to wishing away the body, the irrational, the unconscious itself.

If the dream is anything, in Freud's hands it is a document of the suppressed material life of thinking. There is something morally untethered about all of it – but not thereby mentally untethered; rather, the only principles joining the dream elements together are mental ones, from which every shred of social circumspection and moral concern has fallen away. What stands out is the extreme nature of the dream, with its reverberation of violent forms of inner protest, and its grandiose imaginary reversals. There is a rage for vindication and for greatness on Freud's part, in this and many other dreams, which he characterizes as a childish 'megalomania'. About a different dream with similar toilet themes, he argues that producing a stream of urine in a dream expresses a fantasy of greatness, and he draws on Gulliver's extinction of the great fire in Lilliput as an example, along with Gargantua, 'Rabelais' superman', who 'revenged himself in the same way on the Parisians by sitting astride on Notre Dame and turning his stream of urine upon the city'.[51]

In the Count Thun dream the humiliation heaped on his father – half-blind, senile, faltering, needing help to relieve his bladder on the train platform – seems absurdly excessive, even if based on actual memories of the dying man's incontinence. But it gets even more irreverent! Freud associates this scene with Oskar Panizza's subversive and obscene play *Das Liebeskonzil* (The Love Council; 1895), in which a blind, impotent and syphilitic God has to be restrained from accidentally destroying humanity with his furious wishes, while the Borgia pope is entertained by scantily clad courtesans during an Easter festival. The Zola texts Freud recalls in relation to other dream details include various scenes of parricide and murder. In *La Terre* the father is smothered and then burned alive; in *Germinal* there is a castration scene. All of this is imagined in particularly somatic terms. In one place or another, as Freud notes, the Count Thun dream and its dream thoughts conjure up every major bodily function, while its various wishes – for triumph or revenge – express themselves in graphic, visceral ways.

XVI. — Je croy que ces marroufles veulent que je leur paye icy ma bien venue. C'est raison... Les compissa si aigrement qu'il en noya deux cens soixante mille quatre cens dix et huyt, sans les femmes et petiz enfants.

(*Gargantua*, liv. I, chap. XVII.)

Jules Garnier, illustration of Gargantua urinating on Paris, from *Rabelais et l'oeuvre*, vol. II (1897–9).

The key point is not that this is what Freud consciously thought or desired. He certainly experienced shame, anxiety and resistance to such hostile wishes directed against his father, which, as we shall see, were only uncovered through a lengthy technical labour of introspective self-analysis. Rather this is the world as reflected in – or deflected by – his unconscious, driven by primary affects and desires, inherently pleasure-seeking. This 'other' aspect of Freud's (of everyone's) mind absorbs all the details of his daily life, his total history, and redeploys it according to its own pressing, singular logic. It bows to no external authority (other than those it has already internalized) least of all Freud himself. It is ageless, multivalent, childishly disruptive. Conventional social identities and aims dissolve within it. The dream of Count Thun captures Freud at his most shocking, surreal and subversive; but it also presents something central to his intellectual challenge to modernity: the conscious mind, with its orderly histories and rationalizations, will never entirely control, or reconstitute, these strange, alien principles operating at the heart of the person.

This latter part of the chapter has provided a sketch of some of the ground that lies ahead. The way forward will be through Freud's work with nervous illness, and the patients known as neurotics, or hysterics. In 1883 they were just figures on Freud's professional horizon, but this was soon to change. On 16 January 1884 he wrote to Martha: 'it infuriates me to see how everyone is making straight for the unexploited legacy of nervous diseases.'[52] But there were good reasons for this. As we have seen, there was often little to be done for patients with organic neurological disorders; but the crowds of neurotic patients could offer a lifeline to an impecunious physician starting off in private practice. Two days later Freud announced: 'Today at last I started working on nervous disorders.'[53]

2

Memories, 1885–95

'Hysterics suffer mainly from reminiscences.'[1]

The decade from 1885 to 1895 was pivotal in Freud's journey
towards psychoanalysis. By the end of this period he had near
enough completed his transition from thinking neurologically to
wrestling first and foremost with 'psychological' questions. He laid
the groundwork for a new understanding of the unconscious life
of the mind with its own specific mechanisms – in particular the
repression of unpleasurable ideas. His work on neurosis came to
centre on the problem of sexuality, which would long remain the
hallmark of psychoanalysis under his direction. He developed a
remarkably complex view of unconscious psychological processes,
which he carried over from work on neurotic symptomatology
into *The Interpretation of Dreams*. And, finally, he passed through
various phases of clinical technique to arrive at one of his lasting
contributions to the field of psychotherapy: the eliciting of free
associations as a way to access unconscious patterns of thought.
But before any of this could happen, he first had to encounter the
'hysteric' patient. It was partly to this end that, in the spring of
1885, soon after his appointment as a lecturer in neuropathology,
Freud obtained a bursary to study in Paris for six months. Here, at
the Salpêtrière Hospital, under the supervision of the prestigious
neuropathologist Jean-Martin Charcot, was not only a very large
body of patients suffering from nervous diseases, but advanced

technology for clinical observation that enabled the classification of many new syndromes and pathologies.

Charcot had first built an international reputation as Chair of Pathological Anatomy in Paris (identifying, among other things, aphasia, chorea and disseminated multiple sclerosis),[2] and in 1881 money was raised to endow a new Chair in Neuropathology for him, along with a clinic and histological laboratory, and numerous scientific departments, including one for electro-therapy and a photographic studio.[3] With these state-of-the-art resources at his disposal, and believing the study of organic nervous illnesses to be now fairly complete, Charcot had turned his focus towards the nebulous, yet seemingly expanding, epidemic of 'hysteria'. Considered by some to be an organic disease, by others a functional disturbance or temporary lesion of the nervous system, and by yet others as a form of malingering or attention-seeking, at the end of the nineteenth century hysteria polarized medical opinion. The subjects of Freud and Josef Breuer's *Studies in Hysteria* (1895) suffered from 'neuralgias and anaesthesias of very various kinds, many of which had persisted for years, contractures and paralyses, hysterical attacks and epileptoid convulsions', as well as tics, chronic vomiting and anorexia, and various forms of visual disturbance and hallucinations.[4] Historically associated with pressures arising from the uterus, and therefore specifically with nervous or emotional disorders in women, hysteria's nineteenth-century clinical reframing as a broader neurological issue paved the way for a reorientation of medical approaches and the elaboration of new treatment procedures. For the American neurologist George Miller Beard, the problem was decidedly physical rather than emotional;[5] for British psychiatrist Henry Maudsley, the whole thing was a product of tricks, tantrums or female caprice. 'In hysteria anything was possible,' commented Freud, 'and no credence was given to a hysteric about anything.'[6] Charcot, however, threw the weight of his authority behind the reality of hysterical phenomena, which he considered to be a hereditary condition, indicating a weakness in the nervous system. The task was now to substantiate this for medical science and to co-ordinate and classify its manifold symptoms.

One of the problems was that hysteria could not be correlated either with obvious organic changes (confirmed through post-mortem analysis) or with any observable trauma to nervous tissue – Charcot referred to a 'symptomatic combination deprived of anatomical substratum'.[7] Paralyses to limbs in patients never seemed to match up with possible kinds of neurological damage. Besides this, symptoms tended to migrate from one part of the body to another; even from one person to another – they replicated themselves 'hysterically'. Unlike the Viennese school of medicine, however, with its commitment to identifying specific anatomical correlates for supposed disease entities, Charcot's method based itself on clinical observation: a search for the repetition of patterns of symptoms across a large patient pool, which could provide a verifiable clinical picture. As Freud outlined in his obituary for Charcot, written in 1893, 'The many different forms of hysterical attack were described, and a schematic plan was drawn up by depicting the typical configuration of the major hysterical attack,' known as *grande hystérie*. Hysteria in Charcot's hands thus became a phenomenon like any other in neuropathology, exhibiting its own 'laws and uniformities'.[8]

The hysterical attack was believed to proceed through a number of standard phases, including an initial convulsive or epileptoid period, then one of 'clownism', in which the patient's body performed a series of involuntary acrobatic gyrations; after this came a phase of *attitudes passionelles*, in which the hysteric typically struck a series of more theatrical postures exhibiting the throes of strong emotion, sometimes accompanied by speeches delivered to invisible addressees; finally the patient might plunge into a cataleptic stupor. Besides the grand attack the hysteric could be identified through a number of other features, such as 'hysterogenic zones' (sensitive areas of the body that if stimulated could release an attack) and hysterical paralyses and contractures. These latter symptoms in particular engaged Freud's attention, along with a technique that Charcot had developed which allowed him to reproduce these artificially by subjecting his patients to hypnosis.

The implication was that the paralyses were psychologically induced during a weakened or disturbed mental state. The mental component supplied an explanation as to why the patterns of symptoms so often reflected a lay understanding of how the body functions rather than knowledge of the actual anatomy. Rather than supposing patients were 'faking it', Charcot's experiments with hypnosis were put forward as evidence of an involuntary disturbance affecting the nervous system, one that could be correlated with the similarly mysterious contractures affecting victims of industrial accidents or traumatic railway incidents. The theory was that in both cases – symptoms arising from an inherent neuropathology, and those induced more suddenly through shock or trauma – there was a momentary annihilation of self-consciousness, which allowed ideas to take root in the mind in the form of 'auto-suggestions'.

It was this kind of unconscious suggestion that a limb was paralysed which could be replicated under hypnosis. Indeed, Charcot claimed that susceptibility to hypnosis was itself a characteristic of hysteria. A further implication of Charcot's shift of attention away from female reproduction and towards the nervous body in a state of shock was that men were equally susceptible to hysteria, and even had their own wing in the Salpêtrière. Some decades later, during the First World War, this concern with the male body and hysterical trauma would be revived in debates over shellshock.

As has become clearer retrospectively, much of Charcot's success in objectifying hysteria as a real medical entity depended on the sophisticated paraphernalia with which his clinic was equipped,

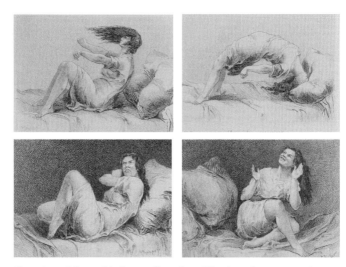

Illustrations of phases of the hysterical 'grand attack' by Charcot's assistant, Paul Richer, from *Études cliniques sur l'hystéro-épilepsie ou grande hystérie* (1881).

in particular the forms of visual documentation that aimed to verify, demonstrate and disseminate the clinical picture. The phases of the grand attack, for instance, were mapped out in numerous graphic charts and illustrations, and the photographic studio was used to compile several published volumes of images of typical symptoms. The methodological weakness here was that the whole system of clinical research operated as a kind of self-fulfilling prophecy. Not only Charcot's interns but the patients themselves often colluded in the reproduction of the typical forms of *grande hystérie* in order to please the master. This became evident to outsiders, particularly in Charcot's public lectures at which hysterics were hypnotized and made to produce hysterical symptoms to order.

The Swedish doctor Axel Munthe set down a memorable account of one of these displays: 'some of them smelt with delight a bottle of ammonia when told it was rose water, others would eat a piece of charcoal when presented to them as chocolate. Another would crawl on all fours on the floor, barking furiously when told she was a dog.'[9] The painting *A Clinical Lesson at the Salpêtrière* by André Brouillet depicts not these public occasions, but a lecture series for doctors and neurologists. Its female subject, Blanche Wittman, who was admitted to the Salpêtrière in 1878, attained a certain celebrity as the 'Queen of Hysterics' and would have been there during the period of Freud's visit. Despite the intention of the demonstrations, such 'theatre' inevitably also fuelled the notion that hysteria was all some kind of elaborate hoax.

Freud's visit to Paris was formative in several ways. Having been initially one of a crowd of visiting foreign students, he plucked up the courage to put himself forward as a translator for Charcot's new volume of *Lectures on the Diseases of the Nervous System* (published in Freud's German version in 1886). This brought Freud more into Charcot's confidence, and, like Brücke before him, Freud obviously idealized the international star of neuropathology, recalling 'the magic that emanated from his looks and from his voice'.[10] Whereas in May 1885 Freud had promised Martha that 'brain anatomy is

André Brouillet, *A Clinical Lesson at the Salpêtrière*, 1887, oil on canvas.

the only legitimate rival you have or ever will have,' on his return
to Vienna he presented himself as a propagator of the new French
clinical approaches, delivering a paper on male hysteria to the
Viennese Society of Doctors in October of the same year.[11] The
attempt was a flop for a number of different reasons, one of which
being that without the whole complex of the Salpêtrière around him
– the performing hysterics, the illustrated charts, the photographs
– the account was less persuasive, and Freud merely appeared as
an uncritical mouthpiece for Charcot's methods. Furthermore,
Freud had no access to his own supply of patients with which to
substantiate these ideas on Viennese soil and simply drew on
material from Charcot's *Lectures*. Theodor Meynert, head of the
psychiatric clinic in which Freud had worked as resident physician,
doubted Charcot's conclusions and objected that hysterical patients
were merely simulating their symptoms.[12] Freud was soon after
excluded from Meynert's laboratory of cerebral anatomy.

Married Life and the New Woman

Despite this initial rebuff from the Viennese medical establishment,
the autumn of 1886 was the point at which Freud grounded his life
as a practising specialist in nervous diseases. On 13 September,
helped by financial support from Martha's aunt, Freud and Martha
were finally married and moved into a new apartment block at 8
Maria Theresienstrasse (on the site of the former Ringtheater, which
had burned down in 1881). Here their first child, Mathilde, was born
on 16 October 1887, followed by Jean Martin (known as Martin,
but named after Charcot) and Oliver (named after Cromwell) over
the next three and a half years. In August 1891 the growing family
moved to 19 Berggasse (now the address of the Sigmund Freud
Museum), where Freud would remain until he was forced to flee
in 1938. Here three more children were born – Ernst (named after
Brücke), Sophie and Anna – the last, born 3 December 1895, would

Sigmund and Martha's wedding portrait, 1886.

later take up the mantle of her father's work and become one of the founders of child psychoanalysis in the 1920s. From 1892 a further flat was rented on the upper ground floor, in which Freud set up consulting and waiting rooms and a study. In the mid-1890s Martha's sister, Minna Bernays, who enjoyed a spirited friendship with Freud and became a travelling companion at times, joined the family in their living quarters on the floor above. Freud was at first mainly dependent on patient referrals from Hermann Nothnagel and Josef Breuer, but he also took up a position as director of the new neurological department at the Institute for Children's Diseases set up by the paediatric professor Max Kassowitz, where he worked three days a week. Freud in fact became an authority on children's paralyses, and during the 1890s published a number of monographs on the topic.

Everything in Freud's personal attitude to domestic relations points towards an emphatic bourgeois conventionality. If his letters to Martha in the years just prior to their marriage reveal his complete respect and regard for her qualities, as well as adoration of her as his beloved 'princess', in a very traditional way her sphere was to be the management of the household, subject ultimately to his judgement. At the opening of their correspondence he had made clear that after the engagement she would henceforth be a guest in her own family 'like a jewel that I have pawned and that I am going to redeem as soon as I am rich'.[13] No doubt this was intended as a fanciful rhetorical flourish, but his response to Martha's interest in J. S. Mill's views on the equality of the sexes was more forthright. According to Freud, Mill 'lacked the sense of the absurd' when it came to the emancipation of women. 'I dare say we agree', he wrote to Martha in November 1883, 'that housekeeping and the care and education of children claim the whole person and practically rule out any profession.'[14] It seemed to Freud completely unrealistic to send women into 'the struggle for existence' in the same way as men.

His marriage was, then, a far cry from the experimentalism of the Bloomsbury set, so involved in the reception of Freudian ideas in England in the early part of the twentieth century, precisely because of his radical theorization of sexuality, or from Berlin in the 1920s, another focal point for the development of a radical sexual politics. According to Freud's biographer, the psychoanalyst Ernest Jones, 'He always gave the impression of being an unusually chaste person – the word "puritanical" would not be out of place.'[15] As Élisabeth Roudinesco has quipped more recently, if one takes into account his decision to resort to sexual abstinence in 1893 because of Martha's gradual exhaustion by successive pregnancies, then 'the sex life of the greatest modern theoretician of sexuality presumably lasted nine years' (though the birth of Anna Freud in 1895 suggests this abstinence was not so continuous).[16]

On the other side of the domestic–professional divide – a literal divide, with the office downstairs from the family apartment – were the hysterical female patients, often characterized as both resisting sexuality *and* displaying erotic tendencies in exaggerated form; unwilling to bow to the kinds of marital or familial duties associated with womanhood, or deemed physically incapable of coping with reproductive labour; described as deceitful, skittish or – as Josef Breuer characterized the patient 'Anna O.' – prone to fits of naughtiness. But the two worlds – family and clinic – were of course not so entirely separable. Freud kept a print of Brouillet's *A Clinical Lesson at the Salpêtrière* on the wall of his consulting room, and his daughter Mathilde recalled: 'It held a strange attraction for me in my childhood and I often asked my father what was wrong with the patient. The answer I always got was that she was "too tightly laced", with a moral of the foolishness of being so.'[17]

Feminist historiography has forever revised our perception of these late nineteenth-century diagnoses of nervous illness as the product of a patriarchal and conservative medical establishment – for instance, the belief that the 'new opportunities for self-cultivation and self-fulfilment in education and work' that were offered to women in late Victorian society would 'lead to sickness, sterility and suicide', or Maudsley's argument that females on the brink of womanhood could 'not bear, without injury, an excessive mental drain as well as the natural physical drain which is so great at the time'.[18] Hysteria, besides being caught in the already involved debate among doctors over its organic reality, was equally the product of a moment of historical transition, the patients being situated at the interface between traditional Victorian values and the emergence of the New Woman. Freud and Breuer in their work across this decade repeatedly recognized – in contrast to Charcot's assumption of mental weakness and 'degeneracy' – that their own hysterical patients included 'people of the clearest intellect, strongest will, greatest character and highest critical power'.[19]

The patient 'Anna O.' (of whom more below) 'had great poetic and imaginative gifts, which were under the control of a sharp and critical common sense'.[20] She eventually found her way beyond sickness by throwing her untapped energies into social work (in 1896 she became director of an orphanage; she translated Mary Wollstonecraft's *Vindication of the Rights of Women* in 1899; and in 1904 she was elected first president of the League of Jewish Women).

Behind this difference of opinion lay the sociological disparity between patient pools: the Salpêtrière siphoning off a portion of the Parisian working class as unfit for work, while Freud's Viennese subjects were often from the upper bourgeoisie (Freud's patient 'Frau Emmy' was in fact Fanny Moser, from a Swiss patrician family and, by virtue of her husband's business in Swiss watches, one of the richest women in Central Europe). However, if Freud was unwilling – at least in the 1880s and '90s – to move beyond conventional Victorian views on women's social position, he was able to think quite differently about what constituted 'normal' forms of sexual desire, and neither he nor Breuer essentialized a woman's fate in relation to her body in quite the same way as Maudsley did in Britain. They were only too aware, for instance, of the relation between hysterical forms of illness and the social subordination of women. The 'hypnoid states', which Charcot had associated directly with mental degeneracy, they saw as often a by-product of certain forms of monotonous work to which women were routinely consigned, such as needlework or sick-nursing. This was especially true for people 'of a very lively disposition, to whom monotonous, simple and uninteresting occupation is a torture', and who were therefore prone to engage their minds in the kind of day-dreaming that left them vulnerable to auto-suggestion.[21]

Much as Freud was aware of the social situations feeding into the disposition towards hysteria, his approach throughout this decade was still heavily influenced by both his training in empirical research and his concern – as a medical practitioner rather than a psychologist – with somatic factors, the intricacies of sexual tension and energetics in the body.

The gestation of his thinking in this period can be tracked in remarkable detail through his friendship with a charismatic Berlin ear, nose and throat specialist, Wilhelm Fliess, who, on Breuer's advice, sought Freud out on a visit to Vienna in 1887. They shared

Sigmund Freud and Wilhelm Fliess, early 1890s.

a similar classical, humanistic education, as well as a commitment to basing their medical research on the foundations provided by biology, physiology and physics. More than this, their friendship, pursued in letters and mock 'Congresses' – held by and for just the two of them in various European cities over the next decade – exuded an intensity and excitement that was both intellectual and intimate. This intimacy was further galvanized by their mutual concern with radical theories of the sexual body, and by the fact that their exchanges were taking place in private – enforced as much by the extremely speculative nature of the theories themselves as by Freud's gradual estrangement from the university.

Freud once referred to Fliess as 'the only other, the *alter*': an individual from whom he gained 'solace, understanding, stimulation in my loneliness, meaning to my life'.[22] Especially in the decade from 1890 to 1900, Fliess became the key confidante for Freud, and a sounding-board for his vigorous attempts to forge a new psycho-physiological understanding of the various modalities of nervous illness he encountered as a practising physician: hysteria, neurasthenia, phobias and his own new coinages – anxiety neurosis and obsessional neurosis. Fliess in turn shared his own speculations on periodicity and bio-rhythms in the human body, on sexuality as a form of chemical toxin, and on constitutional bisexuality (the latter leaving a marked trace on Freud's own theorization of gender). Unfortunately, we only have access to Freud's half of the correspondence, preserved by Fliess's widow and only made fully public in 1985, for Freud destroyed both Fliess's letters and his own working notes after the two fell out in 1900.

From drafts that survived among Fliess's papers one can see that Freud's first attempt to find a general explanation for nervous disorders was concerned with sexual excitability and the depletion or misdirection of quantities of affect. This was by no means unusual for the times. George Miller Beard, the American neurologist who had coined the notion of neurasthenia – the

companion scourge to hysteria in late Victorian times – linked it
to deficiencies in nervous energy, perhaps as a result of the stresses
of modern living.[23] The more common forms of intervention
for hysteria and other nervous ailments (for those who saw
them as more than moral disorders) were thus somatic ones:
low level electric currents, 'galvanization', nerve tonics, spas and
hydrotherapy, sleep-inducing opiates or muscular exercises, all of
which were employed by Freud for his own patients in these early
days in the late 1880s.

One set of questions that preoccupied him at the time was
whether nervous illness was acquired through physiological stress.
In a set of manuscripts sent to Fliess during the mid-1890s – in
parallel therefore to Freud's work with Breuer on the *Studies*, which
will be considered next – Freud speculated whether various kinds of
anxiety, including that experienced in hypochondria, agoraphobia,
vertigo and claustrophobia, were a transformation of accumulated
sexual tension. He at first viewed hysteria itself in this light, as
based wholly on physiological modifications of the nervous system.
The only alternative to nervous illness, Freud surmised, 'would
be free sexual intercourse between young men and unattached
young women' – however, this would make them vulnerable to
syphilis.[24] In a gloomy prognosis, society seemed 'doomed to fall
victim to incurable neuroses, which reduce the enjoyment of life to
a minimum, destroy marital relations, and bring hereditary ruin
on the whole coming generation'.[25]

One of Fliess's more outlandish theories was that the mucous
membrane of the nose was remotely physiologically connected
to the sexual organs, and it was influenced by 'abnormal' sexual
practices, such as masturbation, while excessive menstrual pain,
or a disturbed cycle, could in turn be cured through an operation
on the nose.[26] As Ernest Jones comments, the two men thus showed
an inordinate amount of interest in the state of each other's nose,
and Freud underwent two nasal operations under Fliess's hands.[27]

This particular topic also stood at the heart of a disastrous episode with one of Freud's own patients, Emma Eckstein, in the spring of 1895. It seems that Eckstein may have suffered from irregular menstruation and stomach aches, and thus Fliess travelled to Vienna in February to operate, removing a portion of the middle turbinal bone of her nose, which at that point he believed might provide a radical experimental cure for her symptoms. When the wound failed to heal Freud assumed this was a hysterical reaction, but when it was eventually investigated by a Viennese specialist the surgeon found that half a metre (20 in.) of gauze had been left in the cavity. Eckstein nearly died from the ensuing haemorrhage.

Emma Eckstein, 1890s.

For all the lurid and implausible nature of some of these exchanges, the crucible of the Fliess relationship, labouring at the interface between the body, sexuality and obscure diseases of the will, did bear significant fruit in the form of a theory of pathological defence mechanisms that crystallized around the same time as *Studies on Hysteria*. The theory was concerned with displacements of energy and affect, mis-routed in their passage between body and mind, which prevented somatic impulses from connecting with the relevant idea in consciousness (thus dissociating them from pathways of conscious expression). With anxiety, so Freud argued, a 'physical tension' (read: sexual) increases until it should arouse a corresponding psychical affect, but the latter does not form – either because the subject does not yet understand enough about sexuality, or because of its attempted suppression (because the impulse is alarming).[28] What results instead is anxiety: the nervous system responds to an internal form of excitation, but psychologically the source is treated as if it were a nebulous external threat. Conversely, in hysteria, there is an arousal of *psychical* sexual desire, but through a similar defence mechanism the excitation is misdirected into the somatic field, where it emerges instead as a physical symptom (for instance, a loss of voice, a paralysis or nausea). In 'obsessional' disorders, the same kind of psychical desire remains in consciousness but is displaced from sexual associations onto other ideas, which become obsessive due to the unexpected influx of extra affect.

Perhaps the most striking theorization was that of paranoia, again viewed as a defence against sexual ideas: 'People become paranoid over things they cannot put up with.'[29] A person is excited by something they see (often sexual) but in order to spare themselves the reproach of being immoral, this same reproach, like the affect in anxiety, is 'transposed outward' – that is, other people are perceived as making accusations that the individual would in fact have made of him- or herself.[30] The purpose of paranoia is thus 'to ward off an idea that is incompatible with the ego, by projecting its substance into the external world'. This idea of projection, and the others just mentioned concerned with different kinds of unconscious psychological defences against ideas or desires, would all have a significant future in psychoanalytic theory, emerging as central mechanisms in some of Freud's major case histories fifteen to twenty years later. But they have also provided influential models beyond psychoanalysis. Projection, for instance, was already applied by Freud in 1895 to a political example: 'The *grande nation* cannot face the idea that it could be defeated in war. Ergo it was not defeated; the victory does not count. It provides an example of mass paranoia and invents the delusion of betrayal' (a model, some might say, that was enacted with a vengeance in Germany in the aftermath of the First World War).[31] The same idea – that politicians, rather than accept defeat, may project their problems elsewhere and become absorbed in conspiracy theories – is still widely applied as an interpretation today, both in popular political psychology and in the social sciences.

Hypnosis

Before we can arrive at Freud's fully fledged theorization of hysteria, as set out in the *Studies* of 1895, two other developments need to be introduced. One concerns the experimentation with hypnosis in his therapeutic work. Though Freud had witnessed hysteric patients put into trance states for research purposes while attending Charcot's lessons in Paris, in Vienna there was much resistance to dabbling in hypnosis because of its associations with lay culture and stage shows, which undermined medical authority. For Meynert, hypnosis demonstrated the 'repellent phenomenon of the servile subjugation of one human being by another'.[32]

However, Freud's collaborator Josef Breuer, his senior colleague (formerly also an assistant in Brücke's laboratory), had experimented with hypnosis not as research but as a form of therapy, and in 1887 Freud reported to Fliess that he had thrown himself into hypnotism and had achieved 'all sorts of small but noteworthy successes'.[33] The method employed was again 'suggestion', where the physician would issue commands to the hypnotized patient in an authoritative, resonant voice. But whereas for Charcot the point was to reproduce symptoms, for Breuer and Freud it was to remove them.

The therapeutic use of suggestion had been newly pioneered and re-theorized by another Frenchman, Hippolyte Bernheim, at the Faculty of Medicine in Nancy, utilizing the technique of a local country doctor, Ambroise-Auguste Liébault. One of the key propositions of the practice in Nancy was to challenge Charcot's assertion that susceptibility to hypnosis was itself the sign of a pathological condition, hysteria. Bernheim argued plausibly that 'suggestion' was a ubiquitous phenomenon that could equally be elicited in non-hysterical subjects – an important implication being that what hypnosis revealed about states of mind generated significant insights for general psychology. Freud translated Bernheim's volume *On Suggestion* in 1888 and travelled to Nancy in the summer of 1889, taking one of his patients with him. He later recalled witnessing

> the moving spectacle of old Liébeault working among the poor women and children of the labouring classes, I was a spectator of Bernheim's astonishing experiments upon his hospital patients, and I received the profoundest impression of the possibility that there could be powerful mental processes which nevertheless remained hidden from the consciousness of man.[34]

That same year Freud began his treatment of Fanny Moser, whom he found 'could be put into a state of somnambulism with the greatest ease'.[35] She had been suffering from depression and insomnia for a number of months and came with a variety of hysterical symptoms, including intermittent spastic interruptions of her speech, frequent convulsive, tic-like movements of her face and the production of a curious 'clacking' sound in her mouth.[36] In addition she would interject sudden urgent statements into her talk – 'Keep still! Don't say anything! Don't touch me!' – suggestive of disturbing hallucinations. Under hypnosis Freud suggested to her that she would regain her sleep, and attempted to dispel her various symptoms, on the way wiping out several distressing memories (such that when he saw her later she 'complained that there were a number of most important moments in her life of which she had only the vaguest memory').[37] Work with hypnosis at the same time sharpened Freud's sense of the antagonism between conscious and unconscious forms of willing.

The final element that helped interconnect many of these ideas on hysteria, defence against affect and hypnosis in the mid-1890s, and which formed the basis for Freud's innovative theorization of therapeutic practice in *Studies*, was 'memory'. Back in November 1880 – when Freud was just preparing to complete his university studies – Josef Breuer, already a practising physician, had been called to treat a 21-year-old Viennese woman from the Jewish upper-middle class for a nervous cough, which had come on owing to the strain of nursing her sick father. Bertha Pappenheim's condition would soon deteriorate into an array of striking and shifting symptoms, forever immortalized as the case history of 'Anna O.', the opening case in Breuer and Freud's *Studies*. Her symptoms included, at first, a convergent squint and disturbance of vision, hysterical contractures and anaesthesias affecting her neck, and somnolent states that came on in the afternoon, lasting into the evening. In addition, she appeared to alternate between two states of consciousness: in one she was melancholy and anxious but reacted normally to her surroundings; in the other she was beset

Bertha Pappenheim ('Anna O.'), *c.* 1882.

by terrifying hallucinations.[38] Gradually an aphasia emerged in which 'she became almost completely deprived of words. She put them together laboriously out of four or five languages and became almost unintelligible.'[39] Some of her symptoms began to improve by March 1881, but when her father died on 5 April her condition relapsed – in addition to her somnolent states, she now could only converse in English, and began to refuse food.

The breakthrough in her therapy evolved out of her own propensity for storytelling and daydreaming – what she referred to as her 'private theatre'.[40] In her somnolent state she would frequently piece together narratives based on hallucinations she had experienced during the day – 'the stories were always sad and some of them very charming, in the style of Hans [Christian] Andersen's Picture-book without Pictures.'[41] As the hallucinations became more terrifying, she found that after narrating them she would wake up 'clear in mind, calm and cheerful'. Breuer thus decided to apply this procedure to her more systematically. Coming in the evening, when she was in her quasi-hypnotic state, he would relieve her 'of the whole stock of imaginative products' that had accrued since the previous visit.[42] She herself described the procedure as 'chimney-sweeping', or the 'talking cure'. Breuer eventually interpreted her symptoms as being linked to clusters of ideas produced during her pathological 'absent' states, but he recognized that these complexes could be disposed of if given verbal expression during hypnosis.[43]

Pappenheim's illness had one more twist in store. From December 1881, the nature of her hallucinations changed into a reliving of the events of the previous year – thus in one state of mind she existed in the winter of 1881–2, but in another (so Breuer was persuaded) she was back in the winter of 1880–81, with no knowledge of subsequent events. This meant that the events being 'talked away' in her evening cure were now specific memories from a year ago. It was on this basis, and on Freud's experiences with his own patients in the meantime, that Breuer and Freud would formulate their theory, first aired in a preliminary communication of 1893, that 'Hysterics suffer mainly from reminiscences.'[44] A key episode in the spring of 1882 was the recovery of a memory that supposedly lay behind Pappenheim's inability to drink water at one point in her illness. During a hot summer, Bertha had suddenly found it impossible to drink, pushing away glasses of water as if afflicted with hydrophobia (for several weeks she lived only on fruit). Behind this symptom Breuer unearthed a forgotten incident of a dog drinking from a glass of water in the room of her English lady-companion. This had provoked disgust in Bertha, which had remained unexpressed at the time, but with the retrieval of the memory under hypnosis she was able to vent her anger, subsequently imbibing a large draught of water without any difficulty. 'Thereupon', wrote Breuer, 'the disturbance vanished, never to return.'[45]

Following a similar procedure, the bulk of her other hysterical symptoms were supposedly 'talked away'. However, Freud and Breuer's triumphal assessment of the method in their 'Preliminary Communication' – 'each individual hysterical symptom immediately and permanently disappeared when we had succeeded in bringing clearly to light the memory of the event by which it was provoked'[46] – conceals the fact that Pappenheim continued to suffer for some time (particularly from a neuralgia for which she had been given morphine, and on which she had become dependent in turn) and required several further stays in Inzersdorf Sanatorium up until 1887, after which she began the pioneering feminist social work that would eventually bring her fame.

The genesis of the 'talking cure' – which has gone down in history as the discovery of a new psychotherapeutic method – undoubtedly reads like some mysterious fairy tale, and in fact Bertha Pappenheim would go on to publish two collections of Andersen-like tales of her own at the end of the 1880s. Freud, for his part, regretted that his case histories should read like short stories, which might appear to 'lack the serious stamp of science'.[47] Nevertheless, whatever happened with Bertha Pappenheim in the early 1880s provided only a notional and retrospective starting point for Freud and Breuer's theory of hysteria. The 'cathartic cure' on which it would come to centre was tested by Freud on his own patients, from Fanny Moser onwards, while the meaning of the clinical findings was thrashed out with Breuer from the early to mid-1890s, the bulk of *Studies* being written by the middle of 1894. The final form of the theory, at least in 1895, was that an original experience of psychical trauma or shock, or 'more precisely the memory of the trauma', acts like a foreign body within the mind, provoking intense affects long after the event, which find abnormal pathways of discharge in various somatic symptoms until they can be consciously recognized as such.

Hysterics suffer from memories, they argued, in the same way that painful psychical events still provoke tears long after the original experience. For many disturbing events in everyday life, 'speaking is itself the adequate reflex' – whether as 'lamentation or giving utterance to a tormenting secret'.[48] Likewise, when wrestling to work out the solution to a particular mental puzzle, if someone else supplies the missing answer to the riddle, 'the chain of associations is ended, and the excitation vanishes'.[49] Thus certain forms of conscious experience can by themselves resolve the disturbance caused by pent-up quantities of affect – telling things provides relief, 'it discharges tension.'[50] As Breuer had with Pappenheim, Freud found with Fanny Moser that 'The only way of relieving her was to give her an opportunity of talking off under hypnosis the particular reminiscence which was tormenting her at the moment, together with all its accompanying load of feelings and their physical expression.'[51] Such traumatic memories included her brothers and sisters throwing dead animals at her when she was five; seeing her sister in a coffin when she was seven; and finding her mother dead 'with a distorted face' at the age of nineteen (giving rise to her own facial spasm).

Freud and Breuer agreed that hysterical symptoms were often generated from psychical traumas, related to experiences of fright, anxiety, shame or an actual physical pain, which had been unable to find discharge through the expected mental or somatic pathways. Though in many ways close to Charcot's theorization of trauma-induced states of auto-suggestion, it also marked a double departure from that model. Not only were the Austrians developing a theory of new therapeutic measures, based on psychical acts rather than physiological interventions, there was also a new emphasis on the relation between mind and affect, which formed the principle behind the cathartic technique – disturbances were caused by pent-up emotions needing to be released. However, the two authors disagreed about the way in which such split-off thoughts or affects might arise. For Breuer, drawing on his experience with Bertha Pappenheim, it was hypnoid states themselves that were to blame. Ideas that emerged in such states remained intense, but at the same time 'cut off from associative communication with the rest of the content of consciousness' (a notion close to that developed by the psychologist and neurologist Pierre Janet in France).[52] It was in the soil of this 'second' or dissociated aspect of consciousness that pathogenic memories and their somatic consequences could grow.

Freud's view was somewhat different and drew heavily on his discussions with Fliess about neuropathic defences. For Freud, the dissociation of ideas came about because the ideas themselves were *inadmissible* to consciousness. By 1895 – the publication year of *Studies*, however not at the time of the original casework itself – Freud's conviction had grown that the determining causes of such ideas 'of a distressing nature, calculated to arouse the affects of shame, of self-reproach' were to be sought in sexual factors.[53]

As he confided to Fliess in October 1895: 'I am almost certain that I have solved the riddles of hysteria and obsessional neurosis with the formulas of infantile sexual shock and sexual pleasure.'[54] Freud continued to develop his own version of the trauma theory, paying particular attention to the historical aspect – the complexity of the field of memory, and the development of symptoms over time through numerous interlinked experiences. Thus, in a further crucial way, Freud's work departed from Charcot's through his elaboration of the complex psychical genesis of hysterical symptoms out of a succession of 'partial traumas and concatenations of pathogenic trains of thought'.[55]

Such memories, which often turned out not to be of simple, single scenes but complex clusters connecting over different phases of infantile, adolescent and adult life, required the evolution of an appropriately complex technique, ultimately far removed from Breuer's initial method of questioning patients under hypnosis. Bit by bit, as he approached the mid-1890s, Freud abandoned the use of hypnosis – with one patient, Lucy R., he began to tire of giving the assurance 'You are going to sleep!' only to have the patient retort 'But, doctor, I'm *not* asleep.'[56] With Fanny Moser, he received the remonstrance that 'I was not to keep on asking her where this and that came from, but to let her tell me what she had to say.'[57] Through little moments of recognition like these, Freud slowly adapted his approach to one of encouraging the patient to 'free associate' – which, along with the idea of a 'talking cure', and of lying down on a couch (a technique that had been employed for hypnosis), became one of the hallmarks of modern psychoanalysis. It was probably from about 1896 that Freud came to rely wholly on this method, the same year that he coined the term 'psycho-analysis'.

The procedure is 'laborious and time-consuming for the physician', Freud advises in *Studies*: 'It presupposes great interest in psychological happenings, but personal concern for the patients as well.'[58] The patient must be discouraged from all conscious searching and reflecting – 'from everything, in short, on which he can employ his will'[59] – and instead urged simply to report whatever comes into consciousness in connection with certain associations (Freud likened the state of mind to staring into a crystal ball). The assumption was that the sought-for pathogenic material – hidden or repressed ideas – was in reality lying close to hand, seeking a way out, and if one could only disable the patient's conscious defences then one could meet it halfway. However, the paths of association that might link surface recall to the 'central nucleus' of hysteric pathology were lengthy and circuitous. At one point in *Studies* Freud compares them to 'the solution of a Knight's Move problem, which cuts across the squares in the diagram of the chess-board.'[60] Freud continues:

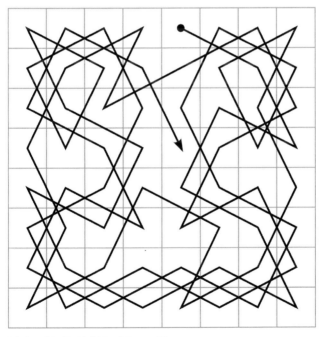

Solution of the 'Knight's Move' chess problem.

Sometimes this procedure, starting from where the patient's waking retrospection breaks off, points the further path through memories of which he has remained aware; sometimes it draws attention to connections which have been forgotten; sometimes it calls up and arranges recollections which have been withdrawn from association for many years but which can still be recognized as recollections; and sometimes, finally, as the climax of its achievement in the way of reproductive thinking, it causes thoughts to emerge which the patient will never recognize as his own, which he never remembers.[61]

Passages like this indicate a clear parting of ways between Freud the physiologist, viewing hysteria in terms of pressures, tensions and discharges, and Freud the emergent psychologist.

In the summer of 1895 Freud was still labouring to draw all his inferences about hysteria, sexuality, memory and the unconscious mind into an alternative 'scientific psychology' couched in the mechanist terms he had imbibed in Brücke's laboratory. Described at first to Fliess as a 'Psychology for Neurologists', and set down mainly in a white heat in September and October, the manuscript of about a hundred pages (now known as Freud's 'Scientific Project') aimed to provide a complete overview of the functioning of the psyche in quantitative terms – 'a sort of economics of nerve forces'.[62] The project combined recent histologically derived knowledge of the function of neurones with the notion of quantities of excitation passing through the nervous system in search of discharge. Freud hypothesized three different kinds of neuronal properties: some that mediated transient processes of sensation, returning to their previous state after the excitation had passed through them; others were capable of altering their state, thus representing the registrations of memory; and a third kind was associated with the quality of perception. From these basic elements, along with the notion of physiological processes such as stimulation and discharge, and a principle of constancy (pressure needs to be maintained at a certain level in order to avoid unpleasurable experiences of tension), Freud tried to model all sorts of mental functions, from cognition and judgement to dreams and the pathological processes associated with hysteria. After a few months of intellectual torment, Freud wrote on 20 October 1895 to Fliess – the only person to whom he confided this project – to announce that everything about the psyche had become transparent: 'from the details of the neuroses to the determinants of consciousness . . . the cogs meshed, I had the impression that the thing now really was a machine that shortly would function on its own.'[63] However, a month later he was dispirited and could no longer understand the state of mind in which he had hatched the psychology; it appeared to have been a kind of madness.[64]

One of the reasons the neurophysiological model had to be abandoned was the sheer complexity of the psychological principles that needed to be accommodated, as well as the difficulty of translating mental phenomena into functional and physical terms. But looked at differently, the collapse of this last-ditch attempt on the part of the neurological researcher cleared the way for the entirely different psychology that was to emerge over the next few years, which is the subject of the next chapter: 'a psychology of a kind for which philosophers have done little to prepare the way for us'.[65] Perhaps even more than Freud's focus on the sexual, it is this growing elaboration of the complexity of processes in the psyche that eloquently anticipates his distinctly psychoanalytic approach to mental life: 'that most paradoxical thing', as psychoanalyst Adam Phillips has eloquently termed it, 'a therapeutic method based on the wanderings of the desiring vagrant mind'.[66] Here ideas, impulses and memories inaccessible to consciousness influence it in unforeseen ways via phenomena such as displacement, projection, repression, compromise formation and so on. It marks, essentially, Freud's shift onto the terrain of psychology proper – a psychology of the unconscious. While an English reviewer, T. Clifford Allbutt, complained about 'the self-revelations of two morbid women' that occupied one-third of the *Studies*' 'wearisome pages', the leading Swiss psychiatrist Eugen Bleuler hailed the book's opening of a 'new vista into the mechanism of the mind'.[67]

The fact that Freud now endowed psychological aspects of hysteria with a depth and complexity of their own – essentially a new terrain waiting to be explored in a new way – is captured in a heroic archaeological metaphor mobilized in his paper 'The Aetiology of Hysteria', which was presented in April 1896, only a few months after the abandonment of the 'Scientific Project' at the end of 1895: 'Imagine that an explorer arrives in a little-known region where his interest is aroused by an expanse of ruins, with remains of walls, fragments of columns, and tablets with half-effaced and unreadable inscriptions.' Their decipherment would yield 'undreamed-of information about the events of the remote past, to commemorate which the monuments were built. *Saxa loquuntur*!' – 'The stones speak!'[68] The promise here was of an entirely different kind of riddle from that posed by neurophysiology: essentially, the piecing together of a narrative and a history, and a work of interpretation.

The next time Freud would attempt a grand theoretical description of the functioning of the mind it would be as part of *The Interpretation of Dreams*, and pursued along somewhat different lines. But the inception of this work was prefigured in another key event, which quietly unfolded in the background of that incredibly productive summer of 1895. This was the dream that Freud had during the night of 23 July while holidaying with his family at Bellevue, a resort on the outskirts of Vienna, and to which he would attribute his discovery of the secret of dreams: that they were disguised expressions of wishes.

That evening he had written out the case history of a patient under his treatment, Irma (or Anna Lichtheim, the daughter

Photograph of the Bellevue resort villa outside Vienna, 1892.

of Freud's instructor in Hebrew scriptures at school, Professor
Hammerschlag), with a view to getting Breuer's opinion. Freud had
managed to relieve her of some of her hysterical anxiety through
psychoanalysis, but she had been unwilling to accept his final
interpretation of her illness (probably that its roots were sexual).
Recently, his friend and assistant at the Kassowitz Institute, the
paediatrician Oskar Rie, had reported that Irma was not quite
well, which Freud had taken as a reproof of his methods. In the
dream Freud reproaches Irma for not accepting his 'solution',
but is alarmed when, pale and puffy, she complains of serious
pains in her throat and abdomen and proceeds to check for signs
of an organic illness. He peers down her throat and sees curly
structures reminiscent of the turbinal bones of the nose. Dr M.
(Breuer) is called in to confirm the observations, along with two
other colleagues (Rie, and Ludwig Rosenberg, also an assistant
at the Kassowitz Institute). Breuer pronounces nonsensically:
'There's no doubt it's an infection, but no matter; dysentery will

supervene and the toxin will be eliminated,' while Rie is reproved for giving the patient an injection of 'propyls . . . propionic acid . . . trimethylamin'.[69]

In Freud's analysis, the dream fulfilled certain wishes: 'that I was not responsible for the persistence of Irma's pains, but that Otto [Rie] was'. Breuer, who in real life equally resisted Freud's turn to a more exclusively sexual interpretation of hysteria, is shown to be 'an ignoramus on the subject', to the benefit of Fliess – 'a person whose agreement I recalled with satisfaction whenever I felt isolated in my opinions'. Freud is thus triply absolved of responsibility: Irma is to blame for her own pains for not accepting Freud's solution; her pains are also organic, so not Freud's responsibility; and they are the result of Rie's 'incautious injection of an unsuitable drug'. Under the guise of a series of seemingly nonsensical events, the dream exonerates Freud, pours scorn on his colleagues for doubting his opinion, and disposes of Irma's medical complaints.

The development of Freud's theory of dreams across the next few years, still in lonely dialogue with Fliess, is reserved for the following chapter. But it is worth noting here how in the dream the distance between patients and physicians, between home and professional life, intimate desire and abstract theorization, has collapsed. Freud's examination of Irma – peering into her throat and requiring her to open her mouth and yield to his 'solution' – is sexually suggestive (at one point Freud sees through Irma's clothes). At the same time Freud realizes that, in endowing Irma with pains in the abdomen, he has conflated her with his wife Martha, then expecting their final child, Anna (Irma/Anna Lichtheim in fact was to be her godmother). Hysteric and wife are fused as one. Understanding the dream thus requires discarding one kind of model of scientific certainty (the search for a causal description of a physical-physiological apparatus), and its replacement by a more intimate absorption in the unconscious interactions of memory, fantasy and symbolization in the mental interior of the person.

In the published account of the Irma dream five years later, Freud would invite the reader to 'plunge, along with me, into the minutest details of my life'.[70] The point is not just that it is *Freud's* dream – one person's particular example – but rather that Freud is acknowledging that the new psychology can only be accessed from within, where everything is subject to the associations of the unconscious mind. This transformed rendering of psychology would have to be consolidated not just through scientific dialogue, or the therapeutic and empirical work with patients alone, but through a new kind of labour, which Freud would pursue through the later 1890s: his own protracted self-analysis.

3

Dreams, 1896–1901

'The chief patient I am preoccupied with is myself . . . The analysis
is more difficult than any other.'[1]

In the Preface to the second edition of *The Interpretation of Dreams*
Freud recognized belatedly that the book was 'a portion of my own
self-analysis, my reaction to my father's death – that is to say, to
the most important event, the most poignant loss, of a man's life'.[2]
Both the instigation of the dream-book and Freud's shift from his
mid-1890s concern with memories of traumas to a psychology of
dreams and unconscious fantasies have a lot to do with fathers.
But it is a hard story to reconstruct, even if the correspondence
with Fliess offers numerous windows onto Freud's rapidly
advancing discoveries during the course of 1896–8. According to
Ernest Jones, *The Interpretation of Dreams* was Freud's major work
and his most original and wide-embracing publication, but it was
not the book that Freud had been expecting to write. At the end of
1895 his new idea for a ground-breaking work was *Psychology and
Psychotherapy of the Neuroses of Defence*, which he set himself a target
of ten years to complete. It is not until a few months after this that
we have evidence of Freud's decision to prioritize instead a book
on dreams, which was finally published at the end of 1899 (though
dated 1900 – as if to mark the dawn of a new era).

Two factors in particular help to illuminate the major transition
Freud accomplished in these years, and both relate to fathers.

Woodcut from a lottery dream-book by Fortunato Indovino, *Il vero mezzo per vincere all'estrazione de' lotti* (The Surest Means to Win the Lottery) (1809).

One is the convergence of memory work around hysteria with the sexual focus of Freud's studies of neuropathic defences. Already in 1893 Freud had been consulted by an innkeeper's daughter while holidaying on the Rax mountain range in Lower Austria. Through a brief interview he managed to establish that her present panic attacks related to sexual advances made by her father when she was fourteen years old. By May 1896, in a presentation to the Vienna Society for Psychiatry and Neurology, Freud was prepared to go public with the statement that in every case of hysteria 'we infallibly come to the field of sexual experience'.[3] This talk was poorly received, but he had arrived at the claim under several different pressures. First, it allowed him to keep his theory aligned with the model that Charcot had used to account for hysterical symptoms provoked by traumatic shocks (even if the latter, unlike Freud, viewed hysteria as essentially an inherited condition). Second, Freud was looking for a ground-breaking insight, something that would go beyond merely relieving patients of their symptoms and instead intervene at the very root of the illness. Given that Freud saw hysteria as, at heart, a defence against inadmissible experiences and affects, it followed that if a patient could eventually recall the original disturbance that set their illness in motion, this might forever dismantle the mechanism of symptom formation. Third, as we saw in the previous chapter, Freud increasingly believed that sexuality was the phenomenon most likely to give rise to a disturbing release of affect. Putting all of this together, he was confident in his ability to tackle the cause of the illness if he could unearth a sufficiently early sexual trauma.

The clinical search for such an original trauma led him inexorably to sift his patient's memories for ever earlier moments of shock lying behind the contemporary symptoms. By 1896, based on associations he had managed to elicit from nineteen cases, he had become convinced that the aetiology of hysteria lay in a number of typical childhood traumas: either the involuntary witnessing of sexual scenes between parents or other adults; or indecent assaults; or the triggering of erotic feelings in the child by nursery maids and relatives who handle them too sensually; or the premature discovery of sexual relations between children themselves. When such early scenes were evoked in Freud's patients' consciousness 'they become the prey to an emotion which it would be hard to counterfeit'.[4]

It was such encounters, he now believed, that paved the way for neurotic symptoms, with the added complexity that they did not do so immediately. Rather, it was only after puberty, when individuals were capable of understanding the import of what they had been subjected to in childhood, that such unconscious memories became retrospectively charged with intense emotions, producing a 'surplus' of sexuality in the psyche, and giving the memory an obsessive character. Only then did the memories become specifically 'sexual' ones – and at the same time intolerable to consciousness.

This notion of deferred effects saved Freud from having to maintain that children's bodies were already sexual – how could such experiences precede puberty? He would famously abandon this position in his *Three Essays on the Theory of Sexuality* of 1905, but for the moment, Freud's clinical work led him to the thesis that 'at the bottom of every case of hysteria there are one or more occurrences of premature sexual experience.'[5] Hysterics thus suffer not only from memories: they are 'psychically inadequate to meeting the demands of sexuality'.[6] He was certain enough in 1896 to believe that this was a revolutionary clinical finding – a neuropathological equivalent to locating the source of the Nile.

However, the paradigm was insecure. Freud never wavered on the formative role of sexuality, but he wondered whether his hypothesis could ever be proved, and whether it was indeed possible to cure someone by recalling such an original traumatic scene. One area of hesitation was the age at which incidents occurred. His clinical material supplied him with countless instances of patients who did indeed remember some form of abuse – in April 1897 Freud wrote to Fliess concerning the case of a woman whose 'supposedly otherwise noble and respectable father regularly took her to bed when she was from eight to twelve years old'.[7] But the logic of Freud's argument committed him to reaching even further back, before the period of conscious memory, towards a notional first instance situated early enough for the experience to have undergone repression. Thus Freud informed this patient that 'similar and worse things must have happened in her earliest childhood'.[8]

But what was the status of such memories? The therapeutic goal required such infantile moments to be consciously recalled – and the experience abreacted – but how was this possible if the incident had happened so early on that it had not properly been formulated as an experience in the first place? Freud's way round this was to assume that the trauma had left a trace in the structure of mental associations. 'Everything goes back to the reproduction of scenes,' he explained to Fliess in May 1897: 'some can be obtained directly, others always by way of fantasies set up in front of them . . . [Fantasies] are protective structures, sublimations of the facts, embellishments of them, and at the same time serve for self-relief.'[9] The building blocks of the neuroses were not events that one could directly remember, but 'memory fragments', 'impulses' and 'protective fictions'. It was these latter mental forms that one could access through the free association method, and from which one might infer the existence of one of the typical childhood traumas. But how to distinguish between a fantasy masking a traumatic reality, and a fantasy that was merely fiction? Adolf von Strümpell's 1896 review of *Studies* warned against giving free rein to the 'fantasies and inventiveness' of hysterical patients.[10] Ironically, the more Freud laboured to uncover an actual event, the more he was going against the grain of the mental complexity that, as we saw in the previous chapter, was part of his original contribution to psychology. But the more complex he allowed his account of subjective life to become – incorporating phenomena such as motivated forgetting, protective fictions and retrospective fantasies – the less likely it was that one could verify a specific childhood occasion.

The pursuit of traumatic memories in his patients provides one key to Freud's theoretical transitions in this period; a second involved a more personal trauma, occasioned by the death of his own father on 23 October 1896. A week later he spoke movingly about the impact on his mental well-being:

Jacob and Sigmund Freud, 1866.

By one of those dark pathways behind the official
consciousness the old man's death has affected me deeply.
I valued him highly, understood him very well ... By the
time he died, his life had long been over, but in [my] inner
self the whole past has been reawakened by this event.
I now feel quite uprooted.[11]

This marks a turning point in Freud's life, setting in motion
a period of acute mental disorientation. At times in the
following year he talked of having 'been through some kind
of neurotic experience' and complained of curious states, twilight
thoughts, and days when he dragged himself about dejected. It is as
if Freud finally joined the ranks of his patients. To cope with these
symptoms he began a period of self-analysis – probing his dreams
and associations for the roots of his own neurotic response, at first
in a piecemeal way, then, by the spring of 1897, more systematically:
'The chief patient I am preoccupied with is myself ... The analysis
is more difficult than any other.'[12] His father's death was not the
only upset in these months. In January 1897, hoping for promotion
to the rank of Professor Extraordinarius at the University of Vienna,
Freud learned that he had been passed over for a junior colleague.
Antisemitism was reaching a new height in the city, and April saw
the installation of Karl Lueger as mayor of Vienna (Freud joined
the Jewish association B'nai B'rith later that year). Business was also
bad, so that financially the Freuds faced hard times; and besides,
there was the slow unravelling of his theory of hysteria, and with it
the hopes for some lasting impact on the professional world.

Early in 1897, these two developments – Freud's attempt to
substantiate the theory of neurosis, and his mental struggle in
the wake of his father's death – merged into a single enquiry. In
February, Freud began to suspect that Jacob Freud, whom only
two months earlier he had praised for his deep wisdom and light-
heartedness, was himself an abuser: 'Unfortunately, my own father

was one of these perverts and is responsible for the hysteria of my brother . . . and those of several younger sisters.'[13] Given his current neurotic traits, the logic of his theory clearly led him towards such an assertion, though he began to wonder at the frequency with which abusive fathers were turning up. In fact, in the same letter Freud himself became an object of suspicion when he reported a dream in which he had 'over-affectionate' feelings for his daughter Mathilde. Based on his conclusions from the summer of 1895 that dreams reveal wishes, Freud even interpreted this as showing 'the fulfilment of my wish to catch a Pater as the originator of neurosis', thus putting an end to his ever-recurring doubts about the theory.[14]

This was just the beginning of a fast and furious set of dreams, speculations, memories and insights that flooded through him as he pursued his self-analysis over the course of 1897–8, and through which he began to reconstruct various forgotten features of his childhood. By October he was living only for the 'inner

Sigmund with his three sisters and his mother at Jacob Freud's graveside, 1897.

work'. It is during this period that he recalled urinating in his parents' bedroom and his infantile rivalry with his nephew John (as recounted in Chapter One). He recovered a formative memory of seeing his mother naked on the journey from Leipzig to Vienna, and he remembered his Czech nurse in Freiberg, Monika Zajíc, washing him in a bath of reddish water in which she had previously bathed herself. Such recollections of a forgotten psychic history proceeded in tandem with shifting insights into the lives of his patients and their symptoms, generating an array of new speculative notions, not only about hysteria but more generally about dreams, childhood and morality, which would form the basis for many publications over the next ten years. 'Ideas dart through my head', he wrote, 'which promise to realize everything, apparently connecting the normal and the pathological, the sexual and the psychological problem, and then they are gone again.'[15]

It will suffice to pick out two major points of arrival in the autumn of 1897. The first was the 'great secret' that he confided to Fliess on 21 September, on his return from an Italian holiday: 'I no longer believe in my *neurotica*' (that is, the 'childhood seduction' theory of the neuroses).[16] He went on to enumerate his reasons: first, the absence of the therapeutic success on which he had been counting; second, the very frequency of hysteria, from which one would have to deduce an immeasurably more frequent incidence of assaults on children than seemed plausible. Most damagingly, if there were no indications of reality in the unconscious itself, then one could not distinguish between truth and fiction that had become affectively charged.

However, Freud did not appear crushed by the collapse of the theory he had been elaborating since 1895. Most likely this was because that loss was offset by the wealth of new insights he was gaining into the psychology of the unconscious, which he was slowly in the process of assimilating. These new ideas revolved not around external events – fathers, maids and siblings indecently assaulting children – but internal ones. For instance, there was his increasing sense of the fundamental ambivalence towards loved ones in childhood, and the presence of incestuous fantasies side by side with hostile impulses – in particular a death wish directed in sons against their fathers and in daughters against their mothers. He found the same wishes coming to light in obsessional neurosis, and in delusions of persecution in paranoia ('the pathological distrust of rulers and monarchs').[17] Some of this was summarized for Fliess in October, in particular, a 'single idea of general value' that had dawned on him: 'I have found, in my own case too, [the phenomenon of] being in love with my mother and jealous of my father, and I now consider it a universal event in early childhood . . . If this is so, we can understand the gripping power of *Oedipus Rex*.'[18] This insight would forever become associated with psychoanalysis, and with Freud's name, though it was not shaped into the theory of an 'Oedipus complex' until closer to 1910.

In October 1897 Freud was still looking for the actual 'scenes' that might lie at the bottom of his own story, which, if they came to light, could resolve his own neurosis. At the same time, he was becoming more and more absorbed by the organizing role of fantasy in the mind. In April 1898 he reflected that he had defined the aetiology of the neuroses too narrowly – 'the share of fantasy in it is far greater than I had thought' – and by 1899, fantasy 'held the key'.[19] Fantasies articulated psychic material, linking memories together with the symbolic expressions of wishes, transforming the appearance of both so as to make the past unrecognizable. But whereas he had previously thought that behind this protective layer of distortion lay a real experience struggling to be heard, the new conception was that our past was through and through a compound of fantasy with reality: 'Reality – wish fulfilment – it is from these opposites that our mental life springs.'[20]

I think it misses the mark to suggest – as has happened intermittently since the Fliess correspondence was published in full in 1985 – that Freud was here turning his back on the reality of the traumatized child. Freud was not a forensic physician refusing to believe his patients' testimony of sexual abuse. Rather, he had put forward the hypothesis – which met with general disbelief, including from his patients – that all forms of neurosis were caused by premature sexual experience, and he had set about trying to ascertain such traumatic scenes through the medium of his patients' dreams and mental associations. Some of these patients had experienced abuse, and Freud never denied that such traumas gave rise to neuroses in adulthood. In texts across the next decade he continued to assert the prevalence of sexual abuse and its connection to neurosis. What he was giving up was the assertion that *all* neuroses were caused by such assaults. On the one hand, there was the lack of concrete evidence in many patients, and the danger of making speculative inferences based on the existence of a symptom (as in the accusation levelled at his own father). On the other, Freud was becoming increasingly aware of the richness and productivity of unconscious fantasy and its associated distortions, and thus of the need to pay more attention to the perverse operations of unconscious desire itself – something he could again testify to from his own analysis.

This completes the account, begun in the last chapter, of how Freud moved from an originally physiological understanding of hysteria, to a psychological one focused on traumatic memory, and finally to a more general psychology of the unconscious. Along the way it has become clearer how Freud became drawn away from the theory of neurosis and towards the subject of dreams – how indeed dreams, not neurosis, became the centrepiece of the *magnum opus* he was ready to publish at the end of 1899. The dream theory seems to have emerged in two phases. There is evidence that as far back as the early 1880s Freud kept a private notebook on dreams, and as we have seen, his patients' dreams habitually provided material for discussion in analysis, primarily for the purpose of tracing patterns of mental association. This first phase of dream interest culminates in Freud's insight, from the summer of 1895, that all dreams could be interpreted as wish fulfilments, and by 1896 he was in fact lecturing on dream interpretation to an academic reading circle for Jewish youths. That same summer, Freud recorded a dream produced by his eight-year-old daughter Mathilde after a walking excursion on holiday in Upper Austria – she dreamed that a neighbour's twelve-year-old son was part of the family and that their mother had thrown them a handful of chocolate bars.[21]

We could think of this preliminary phase of interest as arriving at the 'basic' psychology of the dream, which understands it as a wish, but for the moment this was a side-track to Freud's main research, somewhat disconnected from the theories of hysteria and neuroses. During 1897, though, in the more troubled period following his father's death, the wish theory of dreams started to integrate productively with ideas about defence, repression and symptom formation. Gradually Freud started to find that dreams held 'the psychology of the neuroses' in a nutshell. Dreams became a point of consolidation for new ideas – not only about adult wishes, and infantile ones, but more broadly about the nature and structure of unconscious fantasy. Just as the trauma theory was becoming untenable, the work on dreams was able to take its place as a more promising construct. By February 1898 his self-analysis had given way to the project of the dream-book.

What was it about dreams that Freud was so confident in delivering to the public when he sent the final parts of the manuscript to be printed in September 1899, and over which he joked to Fliess, 'Do you suppose that someday one will read on a marble tablet on this house: "Here, on July 24, 1895, the secret of the dream revealed itself to Dr. Sigm. Freud?"'[22] One thing to note first is that the book bears traces of its complex, untidy emergence as a synthesis between different kinds of investigations, and Freud was not entirely happy with the finished product. For instance,

Martha and Sigmund, with little Anna Freud, 1899.

his decision, under pressure from Fliess, not to include any fully analysed dreams left various points incomplete, or as tantalizing allusions: 'It will rightly be suspected that what compels me to make this suppression is sexual material.'[23] A substantial amount of the dreams discussed are Freud's own, and he was not prepared, in the end, to reveal the full contents of his unconscious desires and fantasies. The book is therefore not a candid account of Freud's self-analysis, and there are frequent caveats, even in the central specimen dream of 'Irma'.[24]

Second, certain ideas that lay at the heart of the self-analysis – such as the nature of childhood incestuous desires – are not given the central emphasis one might expect. The theory of neuroses, and of hysteria, and their connection to sexual ideas, shadows the text throughout, but is also postponed for another intended work on 'Dreams and Neurosis' (ultimately Freud's published exploration of these connections surfaced in 1905, but now in the form of his case history of Dora, whom he treated in the autumn of 1900). Third, as Freud testifies in his lengthy introductory chapter on the pre-existing scientific literature on dreams, many of the general points the book makes were not entirely new. These include the notion that dreams incorporate experiences of the day, their ability to dredge up memories from the distant past, and their association with an unbridled treatment of sexual matters. Freud even acknowledged that the insight that 'ideas in dreams and in psychoses have in common the characteristic of being fulfilments of wishes', could be found in the psychiatrist Wilhelm Griesinger's mid-century *Pathology and Therapy of Psychical Illnesses*.[25]

From this perspective, the demonstration that dreams express wishes, which Freud accomplished with the example of 'Irma' – where the dream exonerates Freud while denigrating the methods or character of his accusers – is not itself the core finding. It neither plumbs that dream to its full depths, nor fully explains how, or why, the 'wish' theory of dreams is so significantly linked to the manifold complexity of individual psychology. The 'Irma' dream simply initiates the topic of wishes, acting as a gateway for the more substantial chapters to follow. Pride of place must go rather to two other facets of the book. One of these is elaborated across chapters on 'Distortion in Dreams', 'The Material and Sources of Dreams' and, most substantially, in the final technical chapter, 'The Psychology of the Dream Processes', into which Freud condensed some of his most substantial theses about the mind: about what is conscious and unconscious, and above all about 'repression'.

At the heart of Freud's dream theory is not a simple idea about our propensity to wish for a reality that fulfils our desires – like the chocolate bars Mathilde wished her mother had thrown into her bedroom. Rather, something more dramatic is at stake: a fault-line in the mind around which dreams (but also hysterical symptoms) act as a kind of transmitter of clandestine desire. Many of Freud's important inferences connect to this. One is the rationale for why dreams need a decoding method in the first place. It is because thoughts and desires laid down in the more unconscious part of the mind cannot be conveyed to consciousness directly – everything must be vetted to exclude any unpleasure that might arise from wishes that, for moral or other reasons, are inadmissible to adult self-perception. Freud famously compared this to the censorship of newspapers at the Russian frontier in which passages were blacked out. In *The Interpretation of Dreams* Freud speaks of the impression dreams give of 'something alien, arising from another world and contrasting with the remaining contents of the mind'.[26]

Another way of viewing this is as a rift between childhood and adult perception. Dreams form a nightly meeting point between experiences of the day and memories and fantasies that exert a separate pressure from the deep infantile past. For instance, in his dreams about Rome, Freud recognizes how his present-day longing to visit the capital, but always-foiled attempts to get there, was a symbol for a number of other passionate wishes, going back to his schoolboy identification with Hannibal and his father's tale about the antisemitic attack in the street, and beyond this to even earlier material, such as the battles he waged with his nephew John, when Freud was three.[27] Stated in general terms, Freud suggests that every dream is linked to recent experiences in its 'manifest' content but to the most ancient experiences via its 'latent' content.[28] The 'manifest' content is what we retain of a dream and usually recollect as a series of scenes. However, this is only the disguised and impoverished remainder of a more extensive set of ideas that represent the dream's 'latent' content – the dream thoughts – which connect to a wish emerging from the unconscious.

However one understands this split in the mind – as demarcating admissible from inadmissible desires, the worlds of adult and infant, or manifest and latent layers of thought – the underlying factor in each case is repression. In 1895, while Freud was working on the neuroses of defence, he proposed that there were specific memories or ideas – sexual in nature – which lay at the basis of a neurosis but were shut out of the conscious mind and forced to remain unconscious (from whence they might issue in the somatic symptoms of hysteria, or as obsessions). But over the summer of 1897, as Freud struggled to retrieve childhood memories of his own, he began to recognize the importance of phases in which aspects of a child's relation to its own body became suppressed – for instance, infantile experiences of toilet training. A string of dreams threw up associations to his first nurse, questions of cleanliness, and the transition from being unashamed of to feeling shame towards the naked body.

At the end of the year Freud started compiling reports that he sent to Fliess, which he called, in German, his *Dreckology* – or 'shitology'. None of these has survived, but we can get a sense of the content from the numerous details about urination, bowel movements and so on that crop up in Freud's dream examples. The reason for this emphasis on 'filth' is that Freud felt he had hit upon the psychological basis of morality. Repression, according to this view, rather than just affecting particular memories (traumas) for specific kinds of people (neurotics) is experienced by everyone as a feature of infantile development. It concerns the embarrassment and avoidance that displace the infantile pleasure in excretions, thumb-sucking and other forms of bodily activity, which then become inaccessible to consciousness. Memories thus fall under the bar of censorship erected during the maturational process – in this sense repression, for Freud, constitutes 'normality' itself. But at night, in dreams, the barriers dissolve somewhat, and the separate epochs of the self come together in a curious colloquy.

In the final, more theoretical chapter of the dream-book, Freud sketched out this new model of the mind in terms of an interaction of different psychical systems: consciousness; the pre-conscious (which holds our store of accessible verbal associations and memories); and the unconscious proper, domain of the repressed. What becomes clear in this final section is the rationale for linking the unconscious so intrinsically to infancy and wishing. Following the assumption that mental processes develop in phases, Freud posits a set of 'primary processes' at the base of the entire psychical system that responds to internal stimuli (such as hunger) by a form of hallucinatory wishing, attempting to replace unpleasure with pleasure by an immediate mental act. This is as far as the very young infant, without motor-co-ordination or language, can advance towards its goals. In later phases, the 'secondary processes' that we associate with rational consciousness – cognition, judgement, reality-testing, morality – overlay and inhibit the more basic wish-oriented operations of the mind. And yet, precisely because they come first, the unconscious wishes 'exercise a compelling force upon all later mental trends'.[29] 'Nothing but a wish can set our mental apparatus at work,' Freud argues, because this is the way in which it was first set up to function.[30] For the same reason, Freud supposed that happiness could only be attained through 'the belated fulfilment of a prehistoric wish'.[31] In dreams we regress to that earliest childhood condition, including a dependence on visual rather than verbal modes of expression.

This general model of the unconscious mind and the split caused by repression is one of the book's most substantial achievements. The other strikingly original contribution is Freud's notion of the 'dream-work', which details a variety of specific unconscious mechanisms that together account for the distorted form of dreams and their nonsensical or absurd content. Freud placed such processes at the heart of his new psychology, which, already in the late 1890s, was broadening to encompass not just hysteria and dreams, but daydreams, slips of the tongue and jokes. In parallel to the dream-book, Freud had begun accumulating material for both *The Psychopathology of Everyday Life* (published in 1901) and his study of *Jokes and Their Relation to the Unconscious* (which did not appear until 1905). All three of these works were designed to illustrate Freud's model of the split, unconscious mind. Part of the function of jokes, for instance, is to recapture an infantile pleasure in nonsense and wordplay, which has since become inhibited by the development of critical reason. But dreams, slips, 'bungled' actions and jokes also share a set of processes that operate in such a way as to distort or disguise unconscious desires, or to mitigate the force of their expression, so that they are less threatening to consciousness. In Freud's theory about the forgetting of names (he published a paper on this topic in 1898) an alien, unconscious train of thought interferes with the intended reproduction of a word, barring it from consciousness. However, certain unconscious associative mechanisms function in such an oblique manner that repressed material finds an alternative, less conspicuous way out. The dream-work, and the slips of expression in the 1901 book, which Freud termed 'failed actions' (*Fehlleistungen*, often translated as 'parapraxes'), show the basic means through which the mind can keep thinking a thought once it has become officially 'unthinkable'. Freud likewise found that 'joke-work' and 'dream-work' were in certain respects identical.[32]

Some of these mechanisms were carried over from Freud's work on hysteria – for instance the notion of 'identification', through which an individual, in a way not fully conscious to themselves, puts themselves in the place of another person and reacts as if they were the other, or vicariously enjoys someone else's desires (or laments their ailments). Hence the propensity – recorded by Charcot and others – for hysterical patients to mimic each other's symptoms. In dreams, however, the concept captures the ways in which identity becomes strangely fluid. There are dreams, Freud wrote, 'in which my ego appears along with other people who, when the identification is resolved, are revealed once again as my ego'.[33] Freud elaborates the same point in *The Psychopathology of Everyday Life*: 'a patient will be speaking of his aunt and, without noticing the slip, will consistently call her "my mother" . . . In this way they draw my attention to the fact that they have "identified" these persons with one another.'[34]

The two most important mechanisms Freud brings together under the rubric of the 'dream-work' are 'condensation' and 'displacement'. Condensation indicates the extraordinary process of compression whereby meaning concentrates in symbols, images or words that are able to represent multiple strands of association in one go. Each element proves to be a nodal point, or junction, between various thoughts. Hence the characteristically 'over-determined' nature of the dream and the reason why the material of the dream analysis is always so much more extensive than the dream itself: the manifest content is 'meagre and laconic in comparison with the range and wealth of the dream-thoughts'.[35] As an example, Freud recalls the figure of 'Irma', behind which were concealed various other persons, including a more favoured (unnamed) patient and Freud's pregnant wife. Irma was thus a 'collective image' with a number of contradictory characteristics – she is 'the representative of all these other figures which had been sacrificed to the work of condensation'.[36] Freud makes a comparison here to the composite photographs constructed by the Victorian sociologist and statistician Francis Galton, who superimposed photographs of classes of individuals (members of a family, criminals, ethnic groups) with the aim of revealing generic qualities in their features: 'The construction of collective and composite figures is one of the chief methods by which condensation operates in dreams.'[37] The same characteristic is a feature of jokes and puns, which exhibit the double-sidedness and duplicity of speech.

But the chief method that dream-work has at its disposal for confusing the censor is 'displacement'. Here attention is drawn away from whatever is central (and perhaps dangerous) in the dream thoughts, instead bestowing greater intensity on those details of minor importance or those only contingently connected to the main theme. Hence the tendency for dreams – and sometimes memory – to record trivial details that can

Francis Galton's composite photographs of members of a family, *c.* 1878–82.

pass readily into consciousness, but which on inspection may reveal links to something more momentous. Through this displacement of psychical emphasis dreams become 'differently centred'. The boldest details of the manifest content are a screen, a decoy. Whatever had the energy to set the dream in motion is more discernible in the meshwork of minor associations that interconnect the dream thoughts several times over, and which Freud more than once compares to a mycelium, the mass of branching threads supporting fungal systems. The same principle is at work in the misremembering of names – displacement leading to the incorrect substitute – and at the heart of certain comedic techniques, when the expected conclusion to a train of thought gets amusingly diverted onto a trivial, banal or ironic side-track.

All these processes are best illustrated by looking at another of Freud's dream examples – this time about his mother, which is useful for the way it demonstrates the erotic aspect of infantile life. Freud would later give much emphasis to this aspect, but in the dream-book it is somewhat under-represented. It is useful, too, for the way it expresses Freud's more complex formula for dreams. In his discussion of 'Irma', Freud arrives at the general conclusion: a dream is 'the fulfilment of a wish'. But in a subsequent chapter he gives a more elaborate version: 'a dream is a (disguised) fulfilment of a (suppressed or repressed) wish.'[38] There is nothing new, he begins in this chapter, 'in the idea that *some* dreams are wishes';

rather, what is decisive is the assertion that even those dreams which appear to express the opposite of a wish – for instance, distressing dreams – are still driven by wishes, simply wishes whose expression has undergone distortion. 'The Bird Beak Dream' is one such anxiety dream:

> *It is dozens of years since I myself had a true anxiety-dream. But I remember one from my seventh or eighth year . . . and in it I saw my beloved mother, with a peculiarly peaceful, sleeping expression on her features, being carried into the room by two (or three) people with birds' beaks and laid upon the bed. I awoke in tears and screaming, and interrupted my parents' sleep.*[39]

This much represents the 'manifest' content of the dream. There follows an analysis that pieces together some of the dream thoughts by following the technique Freud used with patients, and which he describes early on in the book as a 'decoding' method, similar to that employed in ancient divination techniques where the dream is treated 'as a kind of cryptography in which each sign can be translated into another sign'.[40] In the psychoanalytic version, however, the task of interpretation falls not to some priestly 'oneiromancer' but is imposed on the dreamer him- or herself, who must leave aside for the moment the impression given by the dream as a whole and instead break the dream down into its component parts. By following the associative threads prompted by each individual element, the dreamer attempts to retrieve the repressed thoughts out of which the dream was originally formed. Thus Freud finds that the strangely clothed and 'unnaturally tall figures with birds' beaks' recall illustrations in the family copy of the Philippson Bible – the edition with text in Hebrew and in German popular among assimilated Jews. Jacob Freud had inscribed a commemorative page in his own copy of this Bible with the dates of the death of his father and the birth

Illustrations of
Egyptian religious
symbols from
Freud's copy of the
Philippson Bible,
Die israelitische Bibel
(1858).

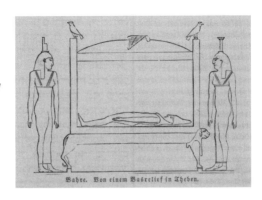

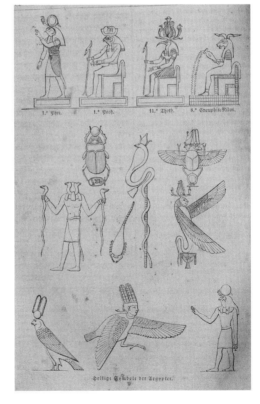

of his son Sigismund. Freud fancied that the dream figures were in fact falcon-headed gods from an ancient Egyptian funerary relief depicted in the volume (the images depicted here are probably the ones Freud had in mind).

In addition, the analysis revived a memory of the son of the concierge – 'an ill-mannered boy . . . who used to play with us on the grass in front of the house when we were children, and who I am inclined to think was called Philipp'. It was from Philipp that Freud first heard a vulgar term for sexual intercourse – in German *vögeln*, from *Vogel*, the word for 'bird'. Freud adds, 'I must have guessed the sexual significance of the word from the face of my young instructor, who was well acquainted with the facts of life.'[41] But the appearance of his mother's face reminded him of another occasion: the peaceful expression he had observed in his grandfather when he saw him laid out in a coma a few days before his death. These words and scenes are therefore all examples of 'latent' dream thoughts – none of them (birds, Philipp or the grandfather) appear directly in the dream as Freud recalled it on waking, but they quickly reveal themselves as mental associations to the material.

Turning the dream on its head, Freud proposes that it was triggered by an infantile wish that had undergone repression – an 'obscure and evidently sexual craving' directed at the figure of his mother. Although this is a dream from Freud's childhood, there is still the sense here of recent events of the day – in this case, playing with the son of the concierge – uniting with more 'archaic' infantile impulses. Freud does not spell this out entirely, but perhaps he intends us to infer that the obscure, quasi-erotic craving was derived from the unconscious memory of physical intimacy in early infancy, now freshly awakened, and suddenly threatening due to the 'sexual' knowledge that had recently been introduced. This sexual thought did not fully enter consciousness. Rather it gave rise to anxiety, on the model of the repressed ideas Freud had written about in his work on the psychoneuroses of defence.

Seeking to find its way past the censorship and making use of the lowered state of vigilance during sleep, the unconscious wish undergoes a number of transformations. For instance, the memory of Freud's grandfather intrudes upon the imagination of his mother's erotic repose; the idea of sexuality is displaced by dying. In a further displacement, Philipp had been telling Freud about sex, but instead of having a sexual dream, the 'charge' associated with that thought has been transferred onto a more indifferent detail – the image of birds, stemming from the slang word *vögeln* (literally 'bird-ing'). Hence, under the pressure of repression, the dream materializes not as a sexual scene, but one involving bird-like figures laying down the body of his mother, recalling his grandfather's prone and dying body. There is also 'condensation' – the dream hits upon a scene that organizes these two thoughts into a single representation: an image from the Philippson Bible (a coded reference to the conversation with 'Philipp' the 'son' of the concierge) in which a funerary relief (the dying grandfather) shows falcon-headed gods (*vögeln* – birds/copulation). Embedded in this very particular and striking, but rearranged, scene, his mother's 'peculiarly peaceful expression' carried onto a bed is now safely detached from the dangerous unconscious wish (though not from the distress it caused).

What stands out about Freud's new psychology is not just the way in which it subverts conscious thinking. This much was shared with other irrationalist philosophies at the turn of the century, the goals of which were often to displace the conscious ego with some more spiritual or occult dimension of mind, whether supra-conscious or subconscious. But Freud in addition opens consciousness up to a kind of clandestine intricacy that, though it appears nonsensical, can be reconstructed and made intelligible if one commits to a more complex and involved notion of the mind. It is in the processes of the dream-work – and along with this the new understanding of symptom formation in hysteria (the unconscious mechanisms of dreams, fantasies and neuroses now being inextricably linked in Freud's approach) – that much of the originality of Freud's work lies. The difference is registered not just in the theorization of new mechanisms applied to thought, such as condensation and displacement, but in the imagery that Freud uses to convey what thinking is actually like. We have already seen the metaphor of Russian censorship, Galton's superimposed photographs and the root system of the mycelium. Other representations include Freud's comparison of dreams to a 'geological conglomerate', or 'pack-ice' – no doubt drawn from his enthusiastic reading of explorer Fridtjof Nansen's account of his polar expedition, and associated with the way in which the dream thoughts get 'turned about, broken into fragments and jammed together' – and most famously the 'rebus', a popular Victorian puzzle in which individual words in a message, or sometimes their sounds, are represented by a visual symbol, a whole sentence being turned into a seemingly absurd procession of images (but easily decoded once one understands the principle).[42] Take any one of Freud's representations of unconscious thought, and one faces something shocking, baffling, comical indeed, but also threatening or offensive to our usual sense of identity, and our preferred sense of 'thinking' – so central and intimate to our functioning – as rational, as straightforward, as transparent to our own purposes.

What marked the rise of Freudian psychology in the early twentieth century was not only a theory about neurosis and sexuality (even if Freud, as we shall see in the next chapter, was for a while associated with seeing 'sex' in everything), but a complex understanding of the twists and turns of thoughts and feelings before we become aware of them. Self-awareness, for psychoanalysis, arises out of a very complex tissue of memory, fantasy, ambivalence, wishing and denial, avoidance, defensiveness, illusion and forgetting, most of which takes place unconsciously, behind the scenes. Conscious choice – we like to assert – is where

Example of a rebus or 'hieroglyphic letter', 1792.

we start from (and much moral, legal and political philosophy as well as consumer theories also persuade us of this fact), but for Freud consciousness is not the beginning of a decision-making process but rather its disguised and distorted endgame. It is this aspect of the Freudian revolution – which for the philosopher Paul Ricoeur grouped Freud with Marx and Nietzsche under the rubric of a 'hermeneutics of suspicion' – that has also given rise to the popularity of psychoanalysis throughout the past century with certain critical modes of enquiry: things are not what they seem; nothing in social, political or psychological life can be taken at face value; we feed off illusions about ourselves and our world, behind which the way things *really* happen needs to be decoded.

Since the publication of *The Interpretation of Dreams*, this same radical challenge has attracted cultural and intellectual aficionados, creative writers and journalistic commentators into taking up Freud's methods, alongside the doctors and psychologists at whom Freud's work was originally aimed. Carl Jung, at that time an assistant at the prestigious Burghölzli psychiatric hospital in Zürich, gave a talk on Freud's dream theory in 1901; the Viennese sexologist Wilhelm Stekel became an engaged reader, and in fact a patient of Freud's, in the same year; and by 1905 Eugen Bleuler, the director of the Burghölzli, was sending Freud typewritten transcripts of his own attempts at dream analysis. Much of this reception – essentially the early history of the psychoanalytic movement – will be covered in the next chapter. But the first review of *The Interpretation of Dreams*, from 1899, was in a literary journal, and one of the first intellectuals to seek out Freud's advice on the interpretation technique (also in 1899) was a philosopher, Heinrich Gomperz.

Thus, right from the start, a non-medical culture of lay interpretation was formed in which 'everyday psychology, salon culture and playful self-interpretations intermingled'.[43] The conflation of the mysterious promise of revelation from the unconscious with a challenging puzzle or parlour game with its own rules and techniques proved attractive to many. 'Is there anyone who has not tried his hand at interpreting his own dreams?', proclaimed Freud's ex-patient Emma Eckstein in 1900,[44] while a feuilleton reviewer, 'H.K.', advised: 'From now on all of us will take our dreams seriously; we won't be able to scoff at them as senseless conundrums.'[45] Over in England, among the Bloomsbury set, Virginia Woolf reported in 1911 how her husband, Leonard Woolf, had interpreted her dreams by applying 'the Freud system to my mind, and analysed it down to Clytemnestra and the watch fires', while Lytton Strachey wrote a psychoanalytic skit in which Rosamund aims to teach her companion 'all about the impossibility of accidents, and the unconscious self, and the sexual symbolism of fountain-pens'.[46] In 1912 the Russian émigré Lou Andreas-Salomé, intimate of Nietzsche, Rilke and now Freud, ably summed up the poetic appeal of Freudianism after attending a lecture on dream symbols: 'in reality no one quite grasps the feeling that his life is lived as if behind a curtain, behind all the conscious events of waking existence.'[47]

Despite the ways in which fascination with Freud's work would grow over the next decade, Freud's view of his situation in early 1900 was bleak. In letters to Fliess he encapsulated his general dejection: 'I do not count on recognition, at least not in my lifetime. May you fare better!'[48] He predicted hard times ahead for his family and his practice and in March complained of being 'virtually cut off from the outside world; not a leaf has stirred to reveal that *The Interpretation of Dreams* has had any impact on anyone'.[49] Inwardly he was deeply impoverished. To cap it all, he sensed a decline in the friendship with Fliess, his 'only reader', whose faith in the work had been such an essential ingredient in the intellectual excitement of the preceding years. What remained in his self-estimation was hardly comforting: 'Yes, I really am forty-four now, an old, somewhat shabby Jew.'[50] Three months later Freud and Fliess

Freud's daughters Sophie and Anna, 1901.

quarrelled openly at one of their congresses at Lake Achen, near Innsbruck, each finally casting aspersions on the other's grand project – Fliess suggesting that Freud merely read his own thoughts into his patients. Though they continued to exchange letters for a while, the intellectual love affair never quite recovered from this blow, and Freud later confided to the psychoanalyst Sándor Ferenczi that he had at this point withdrawn from Fliess something that had been in the nature of a homosexual investment.[51] If 1890–1900 was the decade in which Freud consolidated his theory of the unconscious, the following decade would be the one in which he worked out his theory of desire.

4

Desires, 1902–10

'Ladies and gentlemen, – One would certainly have supposed that there could be no doubt as to what is to be understood by "sexual". First and foremost, what is sexual is something improper, something one ought not to talk about.'[1]

In the late summer of 1901, in the company of his younger brother Alexander, Freud finally broke through his neurotic resistance and travelled to Rome, spending twelve days in the Eternal City, realizing a wish cherished for so long that *The Interpretation of Dreams* is peppered with dreams of *not quite* getting there. Ernest Jones put the obstacle down to another kind of ambivalence: Rome's dual status as the seat of both classical and Western Christian culture, and therefore one of the traditional bases of antisemitic ideology. Perhaps this is why, besides marvelling at the Laocoön and the Raphaels in the Vatican Museum, Freud was above all transfixed by the sight of Michelangelo's *Moses* – an object he would continue to contemplate for the rest of his life, devoting a paper to it after visiting the sculpture daily on another trip in 1912, and returning to the topic of Moses in his final published monograph. At any rate, having overcome one kind of resistance, he returned from the Rome trip determined to deal with another and secure himself a titular professorship at the University of Vienna. His previous application in 1897 had languished in the famous imperial Viennese bureaucracy, most likely because of antisemitic bias.

Now he called on friends, pulled strings (a patient's donation of a painting to a gallery controlled by the minister of education was apparently instrumental) and in March 1902 Freud's position as Professor Extraordinarius was confirmed.

Freud had now to a certain extent achieved the stability he sought in his family and professional life: ensconced in Berggasse 19 amid the warmth and clutter of its solid but dated 1880s furnishings, with Martha, her sister Minna, the six children, their governess, a cook and two domestic maids. Over the next decades – bar the interruption of the First World War – he adhered to a fairly predictable and strenuous working routine: hourly psychoanalytic sessions from 8 a.m. until lunchtime with patients who came six days a week to lie on the famous Ottoman couch that Freud had acquired as a gift from a patient circa 1890. Piled with cushions and covered with an Iranian kilim (a fashionable accessory of the fin-de-siècle) it conveyed less the environs of a sanatorium and more the Orientalist harem: a daybed made for romantic fantasies and erotic adventures. More clinical hours followed from 3 p.m. until the evening meal at about 9 p.m., after which there was time for reading and correspondence at the study desk (Freud often worked until one in the morning).

However, his was by no means a Spartan existence, and time was allocated for the important bourgeois Viennese comforts: the daily visit from the barber first thing in the morning; lunchtime walks and evening strolls (sometimes reading the papers in a coffee house), and cigar-smoking (around twenty a day). He enjoyed cards – in particular the Austrian *Tarock* that was a weekly fixture at the ophthalmologist Leopold Königstein's house, along with two other medical friends (rather than psychoanalysts). This followed his Saturday evening lecture at the university, which was delivered without notes (as Professor Extraordinarius Freud was not obliged to teach and could choose his own topics within neuropathology broadly defined).

Each summer the Freuds would decamp from Vienna, the family usually going ahead in June to somewhere Alpine (Berchtesgaden in Bavaria, Carinthia or the South Tyrol), with Freud joining in July for mountain rambles, fishing and excursions with the children to hunt for wildflowers and mushrooms. In August Freud maintained a practice of splitting off for a more cultural expedition, usually to Italy or the Adriatic coast, often accompanied by his younger brother Alexander, sometimes with his sister-in-law Minna, and later on with favoured colleagues such as Sándor Ferenczi. Despite Vienna's position as a hub for experimentation in art and music, Freud's cultural tastes were quite conventional – he read Kipling and Mark Twain, more sensational fare by Zola, and English

Freud's desk with ornamental mythic and religious figures, Berggasse 19, Vienna, 1938, photograph by Edmund Engelman.

murder mysteries. His great vice, apart from the cigars, was statuettes and figurines, carved ornaments and casts of classical and Eastern deities from archaeological digs, acquired on his travels or via dealers in Innsbruck and Vienna, and occasionally as gifts from patients. He began his collection in the mid-1890s with a set of plaster casts of Florentine statues that were augmented over time by many others – bronzes of Isis and Horus, Athena and Mercury, Neith (an Egyptian androgynous creator) and a stone Baubo, Greek goddess of fertility. By the 1930s the set had widened to include bodhisattvas, Tang ceramics and animal figures from the Americas, gradually filling the available surfaces in his study and consulting room.

Later in life Freud acknowledged wryly that he had read more archaeology than psychology; but then psychology for him *was* archaeology. To his patient the Rat Man he remarked that his antiquities were 'only objects found in a tomb, and their burial

Sigmund and Martha Freud, with his mother, Amalia, on holiday in Altaussee, 1905.

had been their preservation'; like the complexes of a neurosis, their destruction began when they were dug up.²

Even though, by 1902, Freud had a relatively settled life, he had not gained the scientific recognition for his theories he evidently sought. Over in Zürich, and unbeknown to him, there were already faint stirrings that, within a few years, would form the basis for an international psychoanalytic movement. Carl Jung, a junior assistant of Eugen Bleuler, director of the famous cantonal psychiatric hospital the Burghölzli, was tasked with giving a report on Freud's recent writings on dreams. A couple of years on in America, the Harvard professor of neurology James Jackson Putnam would experiment with Freud's methods on hysteric patients at Massachusetts General Hospital. But in the autumn of 1902, when Freud acquired his first circle of followers in Vienna, it was a rather parochial affair.

On the suggestion of Wilhelm Stekel – an Austrian physician with a journalistic flair who had consulted Freud over a personal problem with impotence – invitations were sent out to Alfred Adler (a nerve specialist with an interest in mental disorders) and two attendees of Freud's university lectures, Rudolf Reitler (also a childhood friend) and Max Kahane. Together these constituted the Wednesday Psychological Society, the first incarnation of any psychoanalytic group, who met in the waiting room at Berggasse 19 on Wednesday evenings to discuss various topics on the borderline between medicine and psychology.

By 1906, the date from which extensive minutes of the society exist, numbers had swelled to about twenty regular attendees. These included, besides its gifted young secretary and literature scholar Otto Rank, more Viennese physicians, a musicologist and a music critic for the daily newspaper of the Social Democrats, as well as a bookseller. However, the notes that survive of discussions stand out for their pedantry and factionalism. Visitors were routinely lambasted (though not by Freud) for not being Freudian enough, and departures from the sexual theory of neurosis were characteristically described as neurotic symptoms. Though the topics were often cultural (the year 1906 saw presentations on Wagner, Schumann and Austrian lyricist Nikolaus Lenau) the discussion invariably turned to sex and masturbation: playing piano or violin are substitutes for sexual activity; according to Stekel all lyrics were masturbatory. When Karl Abraham – another assistant at the Burghölzli – visited the Society in 1907, his verdict on the group was fairly disparaging: Isidor Sadger followed Freud like a student of the Talmud; Stekel was superficial; Adler 'one-sided'; and Fritz Wittels (Freud's early biographer and a contributor to Karl Kraus' satirical magazine *Die Fackel*) a phrasemonger.[3]

Sexual Theory – 'Dora'

The major arc of the sexual theory, Freud's great achievement in this decade, was not shaped here, however, in the smoky waiting room of the 'Wednesday Society'. And if these discussions were all that psychoanalysis had produced, it is unlikely that we would know anything about it. Rather we must turn back to Freud's writings – his first three major case studies, of Dora (1905), Little Hans (1909) and the Rat Man (1909), and the ground-breaking *Three Essays on the Theory of Sexuality* (1905) – to find his route into, and beyond, the contemporary field of sexology. The late nineteenth century saw an explosion of scientific interest in the nature of human sexual behaviour, undertaken in areas such as medicine, biology, psychiatry and psychology. Freud's contribution to this work is still striking for the way it overturned some of the major assumptions dominating the field, and for its progressive views about homosexuality and other phenomena at the time routinely described as 'deviant'. But Freud's sexual work has two aspects – on the one hand, the theoretical revolution, and on the other, the psychoanalytic treatment of specific individuals, and it is here that

Freud shows how much the application of his new ideas was still entangled in the more conservative mores of nineteenth-century Vienna.

This was nowhere more evident than in his first published psychoanalytic case study, of Dora (1905), a text that straddles the turn from the nineteenth into the twentieth century quite literally, as the material on which it is based – a brief, interrupted analysis of an eighteen-year-old, Ida Bauer – took place towards the end of 1900, when Freud was still very much concerned with dream theory. In fact, Freud early on conceived of the work under the rubric of 'Dreams and Hysteria', its centrepiece being a pair of dream interpretations, through which Freud traced the formation of Bauer's neurotic symptoms. But the case looks backwards, too, in that many therapeutic ideas had not yet been properly formulated. Read from current-day perspectives, or from feminist angles since the 1970s (as it has been keenly), far from being the jewel in the crown of an emergent theoretical paradigm, Freud's Dora can appear as a textbook study of what not to do: the analyst does not listen adequately, or wields dogmatic authority over the patient; he colludes with patriarchal prejudices against women; and shows an inadequate understanding of his own drive to possess this adolescent woman by obtaining knowledge of every aspect of her sexuality.

Freud was aware of many of the shortcomings of the Dora case, titling it 'Fragment of an Analysis', and comparing it to a mutilated relic recovered by archaeologists – not the least because the treatment, begun in October, was broken off abruptly when Ida Bauer handed Freud his notice at the end of December. Besides this he was painfully aware of the impossibility of demonstrating his own processes of interpretation, because the elements of the psychological puzzle emerged in such a piecemeal way in clinical work that stretched over a number of weeks. There were also serious issues of patient confidentiality: if it is true, Freud acknowledged, that the causes of hysterical disorders were to be found in the intimacies of the patients' psychosexual life – in their most secret and repressed wishes – then the complete elucidation of a case 'was bound to involve . . . the betrayal of those secrets'.[4] Freud was certain that in publishing this case, however anonymized, he would not escape censure. And he was not wrong. All these factors contributed to hesitations that caused him to recall the text from publication in 1901, and to keep it under covers for another four years.

Despite these troubled origins, 'Fragment of an Analysis' remains an electrifying document for its curious blend of science and informality, the physiological and the social, and for the way it disturbs conventional assumptions about will and identity, displacing the psychology of conscious thought with forays into secrets, dreams, buried memories and disavowed experiences. It is fascinating as a window both into Freud's early technique, and for the portrait it gives of a young Viennese bourgeois woman sacrificed to the most egregious machinations on the part of family and society, all in the name of what is good for her. We would not know her story without the medium of Freud's 'talking cure'. The main elements are as follows.

Ida Bauer, known as 'Dora' in the text, was born in 1882 into a Jewish family in Vienna – her father, Philipp, a near contemporary of Freud's, was a successful textile manufacturer but suffered bouts of serious illness, some of them relating to his infection by syphilis in his youth. In 1888 Philipp contracted tuberculosis and the family moved to Meran in the Austrian Tyrol to enable his recovery. In 1894, suffering symptoms of paralysis and mental disturbance, Philipp consulted Freud, who by then was known as a neurologist. In the same year, Ida began to show marked symptoms of a nervous illness, including migraine and a 'hysterical' cough, for which she began to do the rounds of various doctors. Four years later, aged sixteen and in low spirits, Ida was brought by her father to Freud, who suggested a psychotherapeutic treatment. However, it was

Ida Bauer ('Dora') and her brother Otto, 1890.

not until October 1900, by which time the Bauers had returned to Vienna permanently, that she finally entered a six-day per week analysis with Freud – a decision somewhat forced on her, but precipitated by her parents' discovery of the draft of a suicide note.

It is at this point that we get to know facets of Ida Bauer's life in intricate detail – details that, before Freud's work, had never been strung together in quite this way. But a parallax emerges, at least for subsequent readers, over who is authorized to narrate this life, and where its psychological 'reality' lies. On the one hand, we are told that Ida/Dora discovered a new life in Vienna, visiting the Secessionist shows at which the stylistically revolutionary and erotic new art by Gustav Klimt, Egon Schiele and others was exhibited, and attending feminist lectures organized by 'New Women'. At the same time Dora is under investigation as a hysterical subject, suffering from loss of voice and 'hysterical unsociability', which Freud traces back to a disturbance in her sexuality: two ways of being a woman in turn-of-the-century Vienna that did not quite add up.

Despite the concerns already voiced about Freud's dogmatic approach to the material, his view of Ida's hysteria was exonerated in at least one respect: there was indeed a secret thread linking her social life to her ailing body, and it ran via a system of unacknowledged sexual exchanges and sexual assaults. Not long after his original consultation with Freud, Philipp Bauer had begun an affair with a young friend of the family, 'Frau K'. Ida, sometime after, started to receive parallel attentions from the husband, 'Herr K' – when she was sixteen, Herr K had propositioned her while on a walk by a lake, to which she had responded by slapping him in the face. But later in the treatment Freud elicited the details of an earlier incident, in the spring of 1896 when Dora was thirteen. Herr K had used the pretext of letting her view a festival in the town square of Meran from the window of his business to corner her and force a kiss upon her – but she had managed to run away.

These assaults on the young girl, in Freud's view, could act as a sexual trauma, of the kind that in the mid-1890s he had put forward as a possible prerequisite for the production of hysterical disorders. But the network of psychological injuries could be drawn wider than this. For instance, Ida felt betrayed by her governess – a woman of 'advanced views' who discussed sexual matters with her – when she realized that the governess herself had designs on Ida's father, and that her 'pretended affection' for the girl was quickly dropped when Philipp was away on business. Moreover, when Herr K made his advances to Ida on the walking trip, he used the same phrase he had used with a governess in his own household, whom he had previously seduced and abandoned – 'I get nothing from my wife.' Ida was often called upon to look after Herr and Frau K's children, to act as a carer for them (was she being treated as another governess?). She was also tormented by the thought that her father had handed her over to Herr K as the price for tolerating the affair between her father and Frau K. Finally there was no support from her mother, who spent her time compulsively cleaning the house and occasionally taking trips (accompanied by Ida) to the spa of Franzensbad, where she sought relief for the gonorrhoea she had contracted from her husband.

Perhaps the most injurious aspect of Ida Bauer's situation was the family's complicity in disavowing the moral, sexual and marital contradictions that Ida was forced to negotiate on her own. When Ida ran to her parents for help after the incident by the lake, the Ks insisted that Ida had fantasized the whole thing and Philipp Bauer accepted their version of events: there had been no impropriety; Ida was sick and taken to Freud essentially to 'bring her to reason'. It is enormously to his credit that Freud aided Ida Bauer in bringing this tangled skein of secret alliances to light. Not only this, Freud also granted the reality of the young woman's situation – indeed, he is the only adult in Ida Bauer's circle who seemed prepared to do so. Rather than denying the experience, which she could only bring herself to voice at first in coughs and hints and fragments, he reflected it back to her as an entirety.

More problematic are the assumptions he made about her desire. For Freud, the fact that she was not aroused by Herr K's sexual overtures was itself a symptom of hysteria: 'I should without question consider a person hysterical in whom an occasion for sexual excitement elicited feelings that were preponderantly or exclusively unpleasurable.'[5] Freud argued that there were a number of ways in which Ida's desire was complicated, repressed and hidden from observers and from herself. For instance, there was a tendency for psychological wishes to assert themselves in disguise through physical symptoms and activities. Freud surmised that the reason Ida frequently wet her bed when she was eight was linked with masturbation, and it was when that activity was finally suppressed that her nervous asthma arose – the symptoms of the disease, according to Freud, were another displacement of the patient's sexual activity. Bound up with what he assumed were premature, intense feelings of physical enjoyment, was a supposed passionate love for her father – her illness both reproduced aspects of his tubercular ailments, and ensured that parental affection was 'lavished on her once more whenever she arouse[d] their anxiety by falling ill'.[6] For Freud, it was the strength of the repression needed to overcome these childhood Oedipal inclinations that accounted for Ida's subsequent excessive avoidance of sexual thoughts as an adolescent, explaining the disgust that welled up in her at Herr K's embrace.

Freud also pointed out Ida's hysterical identification with the people around her, which further complicated the experience of her own unconscious wishes. For instance, when he learned that for a while Ida had developed an intense affection for and intimacy with Frau K herself, Freud interpreted this as Ida's way of unconsciously identifying herself with the woman her father loved. Behind this were concealed feelings of jealousy, but also – to complicate the psychology even further – homosexual feelings for her father's lover. Finally, as a new discovery of the case, Freud formulated the notion of 'transference', which was to become one of the most significant features in the future practice of psychoanalysis. This concept recognizes that, while in analysis, patients are prone to act out portions of their unconscious fantasies from the past, turning the analyst into the object of emotions that properly belonged to situations in their childhood. In this case, Freud interpreted Ida's quitting of the treatment as the result of anger towards her father (and latterly Herr K), now transferred onto her analyst, for the way in which these former objects of her affection had encouraged her and then dropped her.

There were evidently two kinds of fantasy at stake between Ida Bauer and Viennese society. On one side, from her father and Herr K, there was the gaslighting which asserted that the reality Ida experienced – of family affairs and predatory advances – was a 'fantasy' that she must give up in order to come into compliance with the demands of social life. On the other side, there was the structure of sexual fantasy – including infantile masturbation and repressed heterosexual and homosexual wishes – which Freud hoped to divulge within her, as a substantiation of his theory of hysteria. It would be a mistake to repudiate Freud's account of Ida's symptoms altogether, to collapse the psychical field into the social one and argue that her illness was only the expression of anger and frustration. But it is also clear that Freud was not sufficiently aware of the ways in which his interpretations were likely experienced by Ida as simply another version of the social contrivances she was already exposed to.

Perhaps there was a third 'fantasy' at stake here, which was Freud's desire for a complete elucidation of Ida's psychology, a scientific possession of the secrets of her own recalcitrant will. Not so many years later, when Freud, based on biographical readings, attempted to analyse a childhood memory of Leonardo da Vinci's, he suggested that the artist's drive for scientific research was a 'sublimation' of his sexuality, the outcome of an intense sexual curiosity in his childhood – 'He has investigated instead of loving.'[7] In pursuing his own scientific account of Ida Bauer's sexuality, was Freud – whose sexual relations with Martha were now once more in abeyance after the birth of their last daughter, Anna, in 1895 – exemplifying a scientific sublimation of his own? At any rate, on finishing the text in January 1901, Freud wrote to Fliess, with whom he was still in sporadic contact, to confess that he missed work on the study – which contained 'glimpses of the sexual-organic foundation' of hysteria – as he would a narcotic.[8]

Three Essays on the Theory of Sexuality

If the Dora case remains fascinating and unsettling in equal measure, *Three Essays on the Theory of Sexuality,* published in the same year, shows Freud's progressive, sex-radical face in a way that, even today, retains the ability to surprise. When Freud entered the field of sexuality in 1905, it was already crowded with works by major theorists such as Richard von Krafft-Ebing, Iwan Bloch, Albert Moll and Henry Havelock Ellis, each of whom was elaborating the implications of Darwin's theories of instinct and evolution for the sexual side of human behaviour. For was it not in the sexual realm that human society – even as gilded as that of the Viennese high bourgeoisie – most approximated the animal world? The late Victorian period saw an explosion of medical and psychiatric interest in sexual life, famously catalogued by Michel Foucault in the late 1970s, including scrutiny of the sexual behaviour of neurotic and psychotic patients, children, masturbators, homosexuals and criminals. New terms and inventions proliferated – 'scopophiliacs', 'inverts' and 'sadists'.

It was not that the sexual practices which now came under scientific observation were themselves new; most had been documented since ancient times. What was new was the assertion that there were types of persons – the 'fetishist', the 'masochist' – whose identities centred on their sexual orientation, which was presumed to infuse their behaviour from physiological roots to psychological mannerisms. As the historian Arnold Davidson observed, following the publication of Krafft-Ebing's *Psychopathia Sexualis* (1886), being a masochist became a way of being a person.[9]

At the centre of the new studies lay the assumption that human sexuality was founded on a genital instinct that emerged at puberty and whose task was reproduction of the species. This was 'normal' sexuality, against which every alternative erotic use of body or mind could be defined as abnormal, or even as a disease – a disease of the instinct. According to Krafft-Ebing, 'With opportunity for the natural satisfaction of the sexual instinct, every expression of it that does not correspond with the purpose of nature – i.e., propagation – must be regarded as perverse.'[10] Such tendencies needed to be discovered and policed or curbed in the same ways as criminal behaviour. As Foucault put it, 'legal sanctions against minor perversions were multiplied; sexual irregularity was annexed to mental illness . . . pedagogical controls and medical treatments were organised.'[11]

Freud's *Three Essays* deals with 'The Sexual Aberrations', 'Infantile Sexuality' and 'The Transformations of Puberty' respectively, and each has its own decisive and original contributions to make, but the most revolutionary are the first two. Here Freud reformulated the contemporary scientific understanding of sexual behaviour by attacking its lynchpin: the notion of a genital instinct or drive. Freud tends more often to use the latter formulation 'drive', or *Trieb*, thereby placing the emphasis on an inner pressure, as opposed to inherited patterns of behaviour associated with the term *Instinkt* (though the division cannot be conveyed in quite the same way in English, and I will use the two terms somewhat interchangeably). As an opening gambit, Freud proposed a technical distinction between the 'aim' and the 'object' of such a sexual drive, or 'libido'. Aims refer to acts that could include looking, touching, kissing, penetrating and so on; objects might be men, women, old or young persons, animals, or even feathers or hair. Drawing on the numerous examples collected by Havelock Ellis, Krafft-Ebing and Magnus Hirschfeld in his *Jahrbuch für sexuelle Zwischenstufen* (Yearbook of Intermediate Sexual Types), Freud emphasizes the sheer variety and diversity of the existing aims and objects of human sexual activity, whether as exclusive preconditions of someone's desire, or as temporary departures.

It is then that he delivers the *coup de grace* to the late nineteenth-century theories of 'perversion'. There is no evidence, he argues, for anything so specific as a 'genital instinct', a predetermined connection favouring – or necessitating – heterosexual procreation. This is a social expectation, not a biological one. Hence the decision to outlaw certain practices as perverse, or diseased, is really a social or moral limitation. 'It has been brought to our notice', he asserts with Viennese elegance towards the end of the first essay, 'that we

Photograph from the collection of psychiatrist Richard von Krafft-Ebing, undated.

have been in the habit of regarding the connection between the sexual instinct and the sexual object as more intimate than it in fact is'; these are in practice only 'soldered' together. 'We are thus warned to loosen the bond that exists in our thoughts between instinct and object.'[12]

It is an unassuming statement, but one with significant repercussions that Freud explored in his treatment of homosexuality – or 'inversion' as it was often then termed. Rejecting the idea that 'inversion' was an indication of nervous degeneracy – because it is found in people 'whose efficiency is unimpaired, and who are indeed distinguished by specially high intellectual development and ethical culture'[13] – he at the same time disposed of the assumptions that homosexuality could be reduced to something unitary or innate, or, on the other hand, something acquired merely accidentally or socially. Homosexuality, he argues, has been present in all cultures and at all times; what has varied is its cultural perception. He also rejected the idea of a necessary correlation between anatomy and whether men or women 'feel' masculine or feminine, and in turn whether they are attracted to effeminate or masculine versions of either sex. Here Freud approaches some sense of the distinction between sex and gender long before this was properly theorized later in the twentieth century.

His most important conclusion, however, is that there is no given biological relationship between physical sexual urges and their objects. In some nice touches he turns the lens on aspects of heterosexual love that modern Western societies take for granted as normal and exposes their cultural basis. For instance, why are we so willing to esteem kissing as part of sexual activity when the parts of the body involved 'constitute the entrance to the digestive tract'?[14] The limits of disgust are purely conventional: 'a man who will kiss a pretty girl's lips passionately, may perhaps be disgusted at the idea of using her tooth-brush.'[15] A key element of what Freud was doing here was detaching sexuality from the purely medical or psychiatric gaze, and reviewing it instead as a complex interaction between bodily sensations and urges and more accidental features of development – families, social cultures and traumatic events – which channels desire to many possible ends. Essentially, he was removing sexuality from anatomy and biology and re-materializing it as unconscious psychology, the field he was in the process of making his own.

There was a further corollary of Freud's weakening of the relation between sexual aims and objects, which was the idea that, far from being a unitary instinct, sexuality was forged out of a number of component urges, attached to specific areas and activities of the body – such as touching, looking or aggressivity. Any of these might play a passing, or more significant, role in the makeup of an individual's desire. Aggression might, for instance, be exacerbated in sadism, or take a more background role as the enjoyment of muscular tension. The point was once more to direct the focus away from an exclusive concern with the functional role of reproduction, and towards all the 'extensions' on which many so-called 'perversions' might be founded, but which were in some degree 'rarely absent from the sexual life of healthy people'.[16]

This sense of sexuality as something compound, and not inherently organized to a specific end (other than, perhaps, the binding and release of tension) was central to Freud's redescription of infantile sexuality. Freud was not the first to propose the emergence of sexuality in children. What distinguished his move onto this terrain was his broadening of the idea of sexuality beyond its usual contemporary definition. Now that sexuality had been detached from a 'reproductive instinct', and broken down into component forms of sensual gratification, it was no longer a contradiction to speak in terms of pre-pubertal sexual enjoyment. Freud's core example of the childhood manifestation of sexuality is thumb-sucking (or sensual sucking), which 'involves a complete absorption of the attention and leads either to sleep or even to a motor reaction in the nature of an orgasm'.[17] Though founded on 'the child's first and most vital activity, his sucking at his mother's breast',[18] a striking feature of thumb-sucking was that it was 'auto-erotic', deriving satisfaction from the infant's own body.

On this model, Freud catalogued a whole number of sexual activities and sensations that become sites of infantile pleasure. Children might become susceptible to 'erotogenic stimulation of the anal zone . . . by holding back their stool', or might find their genitals pleasurably stimulated by washing and wiping.[19] Small children, like miniature perverts, were 'essentially without shame', and like sadists they could enjoy cruelty, pity being a later developmental acquisition.[20] Other activities like romping, wrestling or being swung about in the air could set in motion pleasurable sensations that demand repetition.

It was a deft and astounding suggestion: not only are children far from 'innocent', bringing the seeds of sexual activity with them into the world, but what they bring with them are 'the germs of all the perversions'.[21] The thesis concerning infantile sexuality is usually considered to be one of Freud's most shocking – although in fact there were precursors in the field of sexology putting forwards similar claims. But when one stops to examine the idea more closely, it turns out to be one of Freud's most humane assertions. Nothing is medically or biologically 'wrong' with any of the adult practices labelled as 'perversions' because all are inherent in infantile experience. 'There is indeed something innate lying behind the perversions,' Freud admitted, but 'it is something innate in *everyone*'.[22] Perversion, essentially, becomes the model for the development of sexual behaviour, which is initially divorced from any necessary object. 'Conjugal' relations, and reproduction, are possibilities that emerge in puberty, shaped by particular social settings. But by this point, sexual desire in the individual has already had a long and complex history.

Three Essays was not a stable text. New editions were issued several times over the next two decades, each time with new additions through which one can trace various shifts in Freud's assumptions. Some of these additions dampen the radicalism of the original text. For instance, in 1905 there was little in the way of a developmental perspective, other than the recognition that, after a period of latency, sexuality re-emerged at puberty with a new intensity, and more focused on the genital region. In later editions Freud would add more detail on the transition between specific stages of childhood sexuality – the oral, the anal, the phallic phase – which would become the way-stages of much mid-century psychoanalytic practice, as well as supplying popular culture with a new lexicon of insults – being too 'anal', or having an 'oral fixation'. But by emphasizing this developmental account, Freud implicitly – and at times explicitly – fell in line with some of the more conservative assumptions about 'normal' progression.

What would also move increasingly centre-stage in psychoanalysis were the particular forms of attachment experienced in the bourgeois nuclear family. This was the famous 'Oedipus complex', which was to become a focal point for understanding adult psychopathology from the following decade onwards. A question left unanswered at this stage, which Freud began to address a few years later in the case history of Little Hans, was: how does the infant move from being a bundle of loosely organized pleasure-seeking urges to a child intensely seeking love and recognition from its parents? That is, where does the family fit in? For the moment, the nature of the child's primary 'object relations' was only faintly registered in the essays themselves. This absence exacerbates the crude force of Freud's assertions about polymorphous desires that are expressed or hidden in bodies, which lend the original essays their radical tenor. However, as some authors have observed, the missing concern with attachment means that it is hard for Freud to situate tenderness as a dimension of love, for children or adults.

Psychoanalysis – the Movement

If Freud complained about the lack of scientific reception for *The Interpretation of Dreams*, this could not be said of *Three Essays* and Dora. Freud's public notoriety effectively begins here, from street-level abuse of Freud for being 'a filthy old man'[23] (Little Hans's father Max Graf reminisced how it was bad form to mention Freud's name in the company of ladies), to more concerted attacks in scientific circles, where Freud was accused of corrupting the minds of adolescents. Though *Three Essays* did gain some measured appreciation in medical circles – 'no one can read these essays without an inward acknowledgement of the author's acumen, courage, and endless patience in the pursuit of truth,' asserted a reviewer in the *British Medical Journal* – the Dora case quickly attracted opprobrium.[24] In 1906 at a Southwest German congress of neurology and psychiatry, a Heidelberg professor, Gustav Aschaffenburg, led the charge characterizing Freud's methods as immoral.

And yet it was during the period 1906–8 that Freud attracted some of his most talented supporters, those who would become the mainstay of the early psychoanalytic movement and indeed who gave that movement its international basis – Carl Jung in Zürich, Karl Abraham in Berlin, Ernest Jones (moving between London and Toronto) and Sándor Ferenczi in Budapest. Jones, a Welsh neurologist and psychiatrist trained at University College London began reading Freud's work in the wake of Dora and was experimenting with psychoanalytic methods possibly as early as 1906, before meeting Freud in 1908. He went on to help found the American Psychoanalytic Association in 1911, and the London Psycho-Analytical Society on his return in 1913. Besides being a tireless promoter of the Freudian cause, it was Jones who consolidated the mid-century perception of Freud's life and achievements in a major three-volume biography in the 1950s.

Ferenczi, one of the most creative and talented psychoanalytic theoreticians besides Freud, was a Hungarian neurologist and sexual reformer who was inspired by reading *The Interpretation of Dreams* to visit Freud in 1908, thereafter becoming one of his most intimate associates, frequently accompanying Freud on his late-summer trips to Italy and elsewhere. An energetic correspondent and an inventive experimental thinker in his own right, Ferenczi stimulated some of Freud's more radical and speculative theoretical forays. Abraham, originally from Bremen, was another innovative thinker (particularly on the subject of melancholia and manic depression), though characteristically portrayed as industrious but stolid and emotionally reserved. He worked as a psychiatric assistant at the Burghölzli in Zürich from 1904 but resigned his post in 1907, setting up in private practice in Germany where he founded the Berlin Psychoanalytic Association.

But it was undoubtedly Jung, Bleuler's assistant and chief physician at the Burghölzli – which by 1906 was becoming something of an alternative centre for the study of psychoanalysis – who was the most significant recruit. Almost twenty years younger than Freud, and the son of a Swiss pastor, he (like Freud earlier) had become informed about the new French theories on hysteria during his medical training. In the early 1900s Jung pursued a series of word association tests designed to verify the action of 'subconscious' ideas under experimental conditions. In April 1906 Jung made contact with Freud, sending him a copy of the studies, following up in December with his monograph *On the Psychology of Dementia Praecox* (schizophrenia) in which he drew on Freud's theorization of the mechanisms of dreams and hysteria. In the same year Jung boldly countered the attacks of Aschaffenburg against Freud in a written paper, finally coming to Vienna in March 1907. Their first meeting, at which the two men shared their ideas in an intense thirteen-hour conversation, was profoundly affecting for them both.

Thus was established not only a crucial link between Viennese psychoanalysis and international psychiatry, but an intellectual and personal bond that for a few years formed the main axis of the expanding psychoanalytic movement. For Freud, the energetic, charismatic, articulate and independently minded Jung was the 'ablest helper', and the one most suited to continue and complete his work. But the alliance was more than intellectual – their rapidly expanding correspondence recalls the intensity of the Fliess years. Freud admitted to Jung that his was the answering voice he had patiently been waiting for all this time, and in 1909 confided, 'if I am Moses, then you are Joshua and will take possession of the promised land of psychiatry.'[25] As with Fliess, there was an element here of an unguarded mutual intellectual narcissism – something that would leave them both painfully exposed when their ambitions for psychoanalysis began to differ. Jung, for his part, kept a strategic distance at first, particularly around the prominence Freud gave to sexuality as a causal factor in mental life. But by 1907 he had decided evermore confidently to hitch himself to the psychoanalytic movement, and increasingly was caught up in his own identifications towards Freud, acknowledging something of a 'religious crush' on him and, in 1908, asserting that Freud's friendship was one of the high points of his life.[26] Fatefully, he asked to enjoy this friendship not as an equal but as a son – a request Freud symbolically granted at another intense meeting in 1909 when Jung was anointed his 'successor and crown prince'.[27] Within three years Jung would chafe against such 'filial' commitments, but for the moment he supplied the leadership, gusto and professional legitimacy to help secure psychoanalysis on the international stage.

With the addition of Jung, Jones and the others, psychoanalysis was no longer a one-man affair, and to mark the occasion invitations were sent out by Jung early in 1908 for the first international congress of psychoanalysts, held in Salzburg with 42 participants, with contributions from Jung and Abraham on psychosis, Adler on sadism and Jones on 'rationalization', while Freud himself stole the show with a four-hour presentation on the case of the Rat Man (to which I'll return shortly). This was effectively the tipping point of Freud's success. A journal was mooted – the *Yearbook for Psychoanalytic and Psychopathological Research* (*Jahrbuch für psychoanalytische und psychopathologische Forschungen*) – which commenced publication the following year. During the same period the Psychological Wednesday Society was re-established as the more professional Vienna Psychoanalytic Society. However, the most significant development was the invitation extended to Freud at the end of 1908 by G. Stanley Hall, professor of psychology and president of Clark University, in Worcester, Massachusetts.

Freud was to be one among a number of international luminaries to give a series of lectures in celebration of the twenty-year anniversary of the university in 1909. He had had ties to the United States since his sister and brother-in-law, Anna and Eli Bernays, relocated to New York in 1893. But unlike England, home to his elder half-brothers, it would never hold a place in his affections. 'America is gigantic,' he once quipped, 'but a gigantic mistake.'[28] Still, there is no doubt that in Freud's mind setting foot in the new world was a momentous occasion, baptizing psychoanalysis into the future. Though American mores, as Freud and Jones saw it, were dominated by a more 'prudish', hygienist mentality, Freud was acutely aware of the imperative of moving psychoanalysis beyond the confines of the community

Photograph taken at Clark University, Worcester, Massachusetts, 1909. Front row: Sigmund Freud, G. Stanley Hall, Carl Jung. Behind: A. A. Brill, Ernest Jones, Sándor Ferenczi.

of Viennese Jewish physicians from which it had emerged. Already at the Salzburg congress he had sought to assuage rivalry between Abraham and Jung by counselling the former of the dangers of psychoanalysis 'becoming a Jewish national affair'.[29]

Freud did not come alone. Jung, whose association studies had gained recognition in the United States, was invited in his own right, and Freud brought along Ferenczi, who helped in the composition of the talks by discussing them with Freud on morning walks before each lecture; Jones joined them at the American end. The lectures were delivered across five days in early September, with infantile sexuality deferred to the fourth day, by which point Freud had built up a suitable rapport with his listeners, including Harvard professor James Jackson Putnam, the psychologist and philosopher William James, and on one occasion the political activist Emma Goldman, who was 'impressed by the lucidity of his mind'.[30] Freud and Jung both received honorary doctorates, and Freud had the profound realization that, whereas he felt despised by scientists in Europe, over in Worcester he was treated as an equal by some of America's foremost scientists: 'It seemed like the realization of some incredible daydream; psychoanalysis was no longer a product of delusion, it had become a valuable part of reality.'[31]

Freud's fifth lecture, which took up the ways in which sexual energy might be 'sublimated' in the field of artistic activity, captures something of the confidence of psychoanalysis at the end of the decade. The discipline had now travelled far beyond its origins in medicine and the nervous body to colonize a range of new areas, including pedagogy, social hygiene and criminology. At the same time Freud was making forays into the psychology of religion: an article of 1907 commented on the resemblances between religious rituals and the obsessive ceremonials of certain neurotics. In 1908 Freud also turned his attention to the arts, with a public lecture on the motivations of creative writers that engaged with the motif of wish-fulfilment driving popular fiction and linked this back to the theory of dreams, and in 1909 he published his short psycho-biographical study on Leonardo da Vinci.

Psychoanalysis was thus in the process of becoming something more than just a therapeutic measure or even a theory of mind – it was a new outlook on human existence. This much was recognized at the second grand congress of psychoanalysts held in Nuremberg in 1910 with which Freud, accompanied by more than fifty other practitioners, closed the decade of work inaugurated by *The Interpretation of Dreams*, so ending 'the infancy of our movement'.[32] This expansion was nowhere more evident than in the founding of a formal International Psychoanalytical Association with the aim of centralizing, co-ordinating and standardizing the widening circle of activities taking place in Freud's name. In continuation of Freud's policy of broadening psychoanalysis beyond the Vienna circle, Jung was appointed its first president. However, Eugen Bleuler, the lynchpin of the original Swiss connection, soon after resigned from the association in disagreement with its ethos of judging whether something was 'psychoanalytic' more or less by the adherence to Freud's account of psychology: 'if one wants to appear as a scientific association to the outside world, then one can not from the beginning render an opposition impossible.'[33]

Freud, on his side, feared that some of the more radical assertions of psychoanalysis would be diluted now that the field was reaching a wider audience, and already within his own backyard there were casualties of this more formal re-founding of psychoanalysis, namely Freud's two most prominent Viennese followers, Alfred Adler and Wilhelm Stekel, who together had just been appointed as editors of a new monthly journal, *Zentralblatt für Psychoanalyse*, Adler in addition having become president of the Vienna Psychoanalytic Society. Freud frequently expressed his irritation over the pair to Jung – Adler was decent and intelligent but paranoid, 'always claiming priority, putting new names on

Freud's eldest daughter, Mathilde, *c.* 1910.

everything, complaining that he is disappearing under my shadow',
while Stekel was 'a slovenly, uncritical fellow who undermines all
discipline'.[34] More specifically with Adler, there was a theoretical
divergence: Adler gave increasing primacy to conflicts over power
and authority, the so-called 'masculine protest', which he now
placed at the foundation of neurosis, minimizing the contribution
of the sexual drives. Freud feared that 'opponents will soon be able
to speak of an experienced psychoanalyst whose conclusions are
radically different from ours'.[35]

Things came to a head in early 1911 when Adler was called upon
to articulate his position at two meetings of the Vienna Society
and met with savage criticism from Freud's supporters. Soon after
he resigned his presidency and left with nine other members,
eventually to found a new movement and an independent theory,
'individual psychology'. By 1912, Stekel, who had remained
supportive of Adler's presence in the journal, had also resigned.

For the moment, however, such conflicts lay ahead. When Bleuler and others demurred from joining the Freudian movement in 1910, it didn't derail the sense within the organization that psychoanalysis was coming of age – and sloughing off its old skin in the process.

Sex on the Mind

This panorama of the development of Freud's sexual theory would not be complete without examining two remarkable products from the end of this first decade of psychoanalytic development – Freud's case studies of Little Hans and the Rat Man, both published in 1909. These show not only how much Freud's technique had developed since the interrupted analysis of Ida Bauer nine years earlier, but how his view of the ramifications of sexuality in the human mind had come to mean so much more than a reduction to a set of basic instincts. They show Freud transforming scientific psychology into a complex art form, multi-layered with ironies, histories and intricacies, in ways that matched those then emerging in the contemporary European novel (indeed, the Viennese author and former physician Arthur Schnitzler wrote to congratulate Freud on his fiftieth birthday in 1906, acknowledging the inspiration he drew from Freud's writings).

The groundwork for this complexity goes back in part to the emphasis placed on fantasy in the period of *The Interpretation of Dreams*. Little Hans (in real life 'Herbert') was the four-and-a-half-year-old son of Max Graf (the musicologist in Freud's early circle), who in 1908 had been stricken by an irrational phobia – a fear of being bitten by a horse – which severely curtailed his ability to leave the house. Soon it was not only horses that left Hans inconsolable, but cars and buses, too. What stands out about the case, the first child analysis, carried out by proxy through the medium of Hans's parents, was Freud's patient ability to tease out (from hints, dreams, drawings, memories and snatches of reported dialogue) the complex transitions in the mental life of a four-year-old. This includes appreciating the way in which Hans had become self-conscious of his naked body; the effect of the alternating presence and absence of his father; and his recent exile from his parents' bedroom, itself connected with the arrival of a baby sister. These last two events had provoked an upsurge in Hans's affection for his mother, as well as an outburst of sexual curiosity.

Hans, it would seem, was not a trouble-free, 'thoughtless' infant, suddenly hit by an irrational anxiety, but a young philosopher grappling with various threats, burdens and mysteries. What also impresses is Freud's understanding of the way in which Hans's thinking, his attempts to respond to the world around him and surmount various difficulties, necessarily takes place in a medium of fantasy, in which thoughts, dreams, memories and wishful thinking are not always distinguishable from each other. Moreover, Freud recognized that such thinking as 'fantasy' is necessarily exacerbated by the way in which parents seek structurally to exclude certain elements of reality from a child's consciousness.

When Hans's father reported the following exchange –

HANS: 'Mummy, have you got a widdler too?'
MOTHER: 'Of course. Why?'
HANS: 'I was only just thinking.'[36]

– Freud was able to divine that the child was in fact groping his way towards an understanding of sexual difference, which the answer given surreptitiously deflects. Ultimately Hans is also seeking knowledge of where his baby sister (and he himself) have come from – knowledge that he attempts to formulate in a confused way: 'Daddy . . . I was in the bath, and then the plumber came and unscrewed it. Then he took a big borer and stuck it into my stomach.'[37]

The Little Hans case, then, is saturated with the 'sexual' – but 'sexuality' is a complex project. It involves the love he receives or expects from his parents, insofar as this can be experienced as a more or less intense desire, both its absence or its excess releasing a potential for anxiety. It incorporates physical sensations of enjoyment of his own body – including his acts of excretion (there is much here, as one might expect, about 'wee' and 'poo', or '*Lumpf*', as Hans terms it; Hans is a natural scientist of the *Lumpf*). It concerns the distribution of knowledge of human relations and human reproduction, including the enigma over the arrival of his baby sister (also like a *Lumpf*), who in turn has such an impact on the universe of love – 'Would you rather that Hanna weren't alive or that she were?' 'Hans: "I'd rather she weren't alive."'[38] (In a letter of 1909, Jung shared with Freud a similar contribution from his own four-year-old, Agathli: 'the evening before Fränzli's birth I asked her what she would say if the stork brought her a little brother? "Then I shall kill it," she said quick as lightning with an embarrassed, sly expression.'[39]) 'Sexuality' also involves a web of relations with young relatives and playmates, recalled in memories that are often of romping, touching and showing. All these threads of experience are interwoven with each other and plausibly connect to the 'sexual', under Freud's broadened definition, and they form a complex web within Hans's mental life. Indeed, to a certain extent, they are indistinguishable from the main drama *of that mental life*. They are what Hans is interested in, his point of view on events.

Extending the suspension of disbelief pioneered in the Dora case, Freud refuses to treat Hans's curious stories, fantasies and misconceptions as either arbitrary or untrustworthy; rather he sees them as timid steps from unconscious guesswork towards a desired condition of 'undistorted perspicuity'. In his pedagogical work Freud impugns parents for their tales of storks delivering babies, which leave children 'tormenting themselves with the problem in secret', entangling elements of the truth with grotesque untruths, stamped with guilt and disgust. His suggestions for therapy therefore take the form of interventions designed to give Hans enlightenment on issues of anatomy and childbirth. The child's phobia ultimately stemmed from a constellation of misunderstandings, based on things that had been seen but not explained (for instance, a fear that Hans's mother did not like him, because his 'widdler' was not comparable to his father's) and an anxiety stemming from rivalry with his father, and a fear of reprisals, symbolized in the biting horses.

The Oedipus complex (which Freud was formally and conceptually developing around this point in time) comes alive here not as a rigid presupposition, but as itself a piece of knowledge, gleaned very delicately from a mass of observations and interpretations of Hans's little hints and dreams. It encompasses the world as it percolates through Hans's mind, the attentions and movements of his parents, and the objects around him (horses, buses). These come together in a twisted story that Hans is unable to make sense of, but in which he finds himself fearfully caught. Freud's strategy for releasing Hans from his phobia, on the one occasion when they met to pursue the therapy face to face, is both masterful and touching:

> I then disclosed to him that he was afraid of his father, precisely because he was so fond of his mother. It must be, I told him, that he thought his father was angry with him on that account; but this was not so, his father was fond of him in spite of it, and he might admit everything to him without any fear. Long before he was in the world, I went on, I had known that a little Hans would come who would be so fond of his mother that he would be bound to feel afraid of his father because of it; and I had told his father this.[40]

The therapy thus turns on the attempt to bring aspects of psychology that function unconsciously, in a confused and excessive way, into the prosaic light of day, so that conflicts can be understood and defused without necessarily being dispelled. Though aspects of Hans's disorder persisted for a little while, it was no longer expressed as 'fear' but rather in 'the normal instinct for asking questions'.[41]

Part of the rationale for publicly presenting the Hans case was to show at first hand, in a child, the wayward intersection of sexual desire, fantasy and thought that psychoanalysis posited at the heart of unconscious psychology and neurotic illness. The case of the Rat Man – whose analysis, that of the 29-year-old Viennese lawyer Ernst Lanzer, was unfolding to a certain extent simultaneously during 1907–8 – was designed to show how such excessive, confused and fantastical acts of thought in infancy could return to bewilder and compromise the life of an adult. As Freud put it in the Hans case: a thing that hasn't been understood reappears, like an 'unlaid ghost'.[42]

There is no space here to unravel fully the story of the Rat Man that serves as Freud's illustration of the mechanisms of obsessional neurosis, to set beside his studies of hysteria (Dora) and phobia (Hans). Its touches of absurdity mingled with horror make it a classic of literature as well as psychoanalysis – Jung regretted 'from the bottom of [his] heart that [he] didn't write it'.[43] Everything again hinges on sexuality, but not as we would normally understand it. At one level, Lanzer was plagued by an inability to decide whom to marry out of two possible partners, and in addition an increasingly drawn-out vacillation – between intense passion and indifference – in relation to the one he appeared to be actually in love with. But besides this he was beset by fears that some misfortune would befall her or his own father (despite the latter being already deceased), and violent, sometimes suicidal compulsions, as well as self-imposed prohibitions over quite trivial matters: 'He had wasted years, he told me, in fighting against these ideas of his, and in this way had lost much ground in the course of his life.'[44] Freud is interested in tracing how the whole of Lanzer's neurosis – built on ambivalence and complicated counter-wishes, which had an intermittent presence in his mind throughout his life – could be traced back to a turbulent period in infancy. They derived ultimately from a premature fascination with the sexual (Lanzer was seduced by his governess when he was four), as well as extreme hostility towards the interventions of his father: 'thoughts about his father's death had occupied his mind when he was a small boy with unusual and undue intensity'.[45]

It is not just the chain of sexual experience linking infancy to adulthood that concerns Freud, nor the entanglement of love and aggression (fast emerging as the two component poles of the Oedipus complex, and which, in Lanzer's case, leads to a fascinating but disturbed emotional compound). It is also the displacement of Lanzer's intense childhood concern with sexuality onto his mental operations as a whole. One of Freud's most original accomplishments here, as in Little Hans, is his reconstruction of infantile 'megalomania', in the sense he had already elicited from his own childish behaviour in *The Interpretation of Dreams*. In the Rat Man case this concerns the belief in the 'omnipotence of thoughts'. Lanzer's unconscious thought – 'If I have this wish to see a woman naked, my father will be bound to die' – proves essential to the structure of his illness, along with the morbid idea that his parents could hear his thoughts.[46]

What Freud proposes here is that thinking itself, invested with erotic and aggressive qualities, has become 'sexualized': 'the sexual pleasure which is normally attached to the content of thought becomes shifted on to the act of thinking itself'.[47] Hence Lanzer's compulsive thoughts, as well as his need for prevarication and doubt – for lingering over preparatory acts – *are* the expression of his sexuality, or have become so, in the same way that Dora's sexual life consisted in her physical ailments. This topic of the 'omnipotence of thoughts', thinking contaminated by desire, and the mythic quality that adheres to rationality itself, forms a frame for understanding much of Freud's mature psychology as it unfolds in the following decades.

5

Mythologies, 1910–23

'It may perhaps seem to you as though our theories are a kind of
mythology and, in the present case, not even an agreeable one.'[1]

This chapter follows the thread of Freud's life and the development
of psychoanalysis beyond the formative first decade of the 1900s
that ended with the consolidation of some of its more fundamental
tenets – repression, infantile sexuality and the Oedipus complex
– as well as the underpinnings of an international movement with
off-shoots in Zürich and Berlin, soon to be followed by London,
New York and Budapest. The many key developments that came
after this, only some of which can be reviewed here, belong to a
second phase that, within a few years, would be sharply demarcated
from the first – not only by the breaks with Alfred Adler, Wilhelm
Stekel and then Carl Jung, but also by the First World War. In
addition there were dramatic shifts going on in the very fabric
of psychoanalytic thinking through which new points of focus
emerged, concepts were developed and contested, and the general
framework of the psychoanalytic paradigm – including Freud's
theory of the drives, the ego and the unconscious – fell apart more
than once.

All these developments are here placed under the rubric of
'mythologies', because myth was a burgeoning area in which
psychoanalysts found a distinctive voice as a counterpart to medical
and therapeutic activities. Already in 1908, in his talk on creative

writing, Freud had alluded to myths, legends and fairy tales as a popular treasure-house for expressions of unconscious desire.[2] In 1909 Jung was immersing himself in works on ancient symbolism and confiding to Freud that 'archaeology, or rather mythology has got me in its grip'.[3] In the same year Otto Rank published his seminal study on myths of the birth of heroes, and Karl Abraham one on Prometheus.

The extension of psychoanalysis onto myth was a way, perhaps, of making Freud's seemingly toxic message more culturally palatable. But there were also methodological reasons: where the fragmentary and indelibly personal nature of reports on dreams and clinical symptoms remained unpersuasive for large sections of the medical community, literature, folklore and mythology provided a more generic terrain on which to demonstrate the novel interpretive techniques. Myth was thus also a step in the direction of universalization – an attempt at establishing certain kinds of symbols, particularly sexual ones, as ubiquitous across cultures. At the 1910 Nuremberg congress Stekel tabled a motion to establish a committee for 'collective research on the symbolism of dreams and neuroses'.[4] The evidence gathered soon found its way into the new psychoanalytic journals, above all *Imago*, founded in 1912 and edited by Hanns Sachs and Otto Rank, which was devoted to the application of psychoanalysis to cultural material. The same year saw the completion of Jung's *Transformations and Symbols of the Libido*, a magnum opus on myth and neurosis that had been gestating since 1909, as well as the publication of the first of four essays that would comprise Freud's *Totem and Taboo* (1912–13), his own answering effort to consolidate psychoanalysis on the grounds of primitive anthropology.

A further twist to the fortunes of myth in psychoanalysis emerged in the second decade of the twentieth century, which was the growing supposition of a universal unconscious symbolism inherited from more archaic layers of human culture. Jung was

Illustration from George Nicol (attrib.), *An Hour at Bearwood: The Wolf and the Seven Kids* (1838).

perhaps the first to become interested in this phylogenetic basis for the theory of neurosis, but Freud was soon adopting a similar view of hysteria and obsessional neurosis as atavistic recollections of experiences from the evolution of the species. This kind of conjecture in Freud's work, though never wholly dominating his approach to psychoanalysis, would become more pronounced over time. Most famously it emerged in the case history of the 'Wolf Man', which Freud was drafting in 1914. Sergei Pankejeff was a wealthy Russian who suffered from a severe neurosis dating back to when he was four years old. At that time his hysterical anxiety manifested in an animal phobia encapsulated in a dream of wolves watching him from the branches of a tree. Together, Freud and Pankejeff traced these images back to illustrations of fairy tales – 'Little Red Riding Hood' and 'The Wolf and the Seven Little Kids' – but also to a supposed 'primal scene', in which the child at an even earlier age had slept in his parents' bedroom and woken to witness a sexual scene, one interpreted by the child as violent animalistic movement. Freud wrestled with the fact that, though the scene seemed necessary for making sense of the neurosis, it was a 'construction' of the analysis, rather than an actual memory.

He finally resolved the issue by arguing that, whether or not the scene in Pankejeff's case had been a fantasy or a real experience, it was anyway an atavistic recollection, embedded in human culture, equally surfacing in myths and fairy tales: 'These scenes of observing parental intercourse, of being seduced in childhood, and of being threatened with castration are unquestionably an inherited endowment . . . but they may just as easily be acquired by personal experience.'[5] If the turn to myth appears at first as a step away from medical science into cultural interpretation, it equally took Freud nearer to a thesis of evolutionary psychology.

Psychosis

Besides providing a storehouse of 'collective fantasies', mythology also designates several other developments in the period after 1910. One of these is Freud's turn from hysteria to psychosis. Jung's lead was again significant here. Physicians not attached to psychiatric institutions had little chance to observe patients suffering from the more severe forms of psychopathology, but at the Burghölzli Jung was confronted with such cases on a daily basis and by 1907 was treating the deliria of psychotic patients as meaningful and interpretable in the same way as dreams. Central to Freud's own engagement with psychotic experience was the remarkable autobiographical account by a German judge, Daniel Paul Schreber, of his severe mental breakdown, published in 1903 as *Memoirs of My Nervous Illness*. Freud took this work with him as summer reading during his travels in Sicily with Sándor Ferenczi in 1910, and in the final months of that year wrote an analysis of Schreber's illness in the form of a case history.

A short list of some of Schreber's symptoms quickly establishes a parallel to the delusional work of dreams. Presenting originally with hypochondriacal ideas – he was dying, his brain was getting soft – Schreber's illness developed into something markedly more deranged: he was persecuted, abused, he had no stomach or intestines and 'used sometimes to swallow part of his own larynx with his food'.[6] Gradually what emerged was a grander religious conception: the world was suffused with 'nerve-rays' and was being destroyed because the rays of God had become entangled with those of his own body. Above all, his body was being transformed into that of a woman: 'He has a feeling that enormous numbers of "female nerves" have already passed over into his body, and out of them a new race of men will proceed, through a process of direct impregnation by God.'[7]

Schreber fashioned his delusion into a comprehensive mythic structure in order to make sense of his reality. It was this 'world-building' capacity that fascinated Freud, as it fitted with his earlier speculations about the operation of paranoia. According to Freud, the cause of Schreber's illness was an idea that, as noted in the memoir, had popped into his mind shortly before his major breakdown: 'after all it really must be very nice to be a woman submitting to the act of copulation.'[8] This idea, which Freud interpreted as a repressed homosexual desire, was the 'nuclear complex' of the case, which at first aroused intense internal resistance. In the ensuing defensive struggle in his mind, Schreber's wish was transformed into a sexual delusion of persecution: the person he longed for now became his tormentor – hence Schreber's initial conviction of a conspiracy to murder his soul. As the struggle continued, the defences became more cataclysmic, setting off a fantasy that the world had been destroyed. Freud speculated that the libido defensively withdrawn from external objects became instead attached to Schreber himself, giving rise to megalomania.

Interestingly, for Freud, this latter, grandly mythopoeic phase of the delusion, in which Schreber was to be impregnated at God's behest, was not the nadir of mental disintegration but an attempt to rebuild the universe in a form that could accommodate his original 'feminine' desire. The paranoiac builds the world up in delusional form in order to live in it again; it is a work of recovery.[9]

Paranoid psychosis was not only myth-*like*. Both Jung and Freud speculated that such unusual fantasies might in some obscure way reflect the structures of archaic myth. In the autumn of 1910 Jung had been immersing himself in Iranian archaeology and unearthing parallels to the fantasies he had found in patient material. By the following summer he was more convinced that introversion in delusional fantasy could lead 'to a loosening up of the historical layers of the unconscious'.[10] In relation to Schreber, both Freud and Jung surmised that a portion of his delusions was reproducing an ancient myth complex equating the Sun with a deified father. In a 'Postscript' to the case, which Freud delivered at the third congress of the International Psychoanalytical Association in Weimar, in September 1911, he brought forward the solar myth as supporting evidence for Jung's assertion that 'the mythopoeic forces of mankind are not extinct, but . . . to this very day they give rise in the neuroses to the same psychical products as in the remotest past ages.'[11] In dreams and mental disturbance, Freud was now prepared to say, we come not only upon the emotional life of the child, but equally upon 'primitive man'.

Narcissism

A second new development that confronted Freud with the hold of myth over the psyche was the concept of narcissism. This had emerged as a passing focus in the Schreber case, when Freud suggested that the libido normally directed towards people might be retracted and attached to one's own self, giving rise to megalomania as a sexual over-valuation of the ego. In his work up until 1910, the ego had stood for the pole of rational self-consciousness and moral judgement, against which Freud had elaborated the more recalcitrant and hidden principles of the unconscious. The ego itself was rarely in the spotlight, except where Freud attributed to it some role in the censorship of unwanted ideas. But with the concept of narcissism he conceded something that would revolutionize his model of the mind.

Freud had first employed the term 'narcissism' to resolve the issue of how the child moves from its original condition of polymorphous auto-eroticism towards the kind of 'object love' associated with attachments to parents and the unfolding of the Oedipus complex. The answer was that the child takes him- or herself as a first love object, and only thereafter moves on to loving another person. This was the stage of 'normal narcissism' that everyone passes through in infancy. In 1914, consolidating various leads about narcissism in his recent papers, Freud now acknowledged that whereas auto-eroticism is there from the start, the ego emerges only gradually from an original condition of narcissism, of self-love, to which it will remain forever susceptible, and indeed aims vigorously to recover. The question now was not under what conditions the rational ego might be assaulted by unconscious desires, but how was it that the ego was able to move beyond narcissism in the first place – beyond its position as 'His Majesty the Baby', as Freud liked to call it, alluding to a popular turn-of-the-century print.[12]

As Freud started to consider the relations between the ego and self-love more closely, narcissism became a thread linking everyone to everything. It was the libidinal counterpart to the self-preservative drive, 'which may justifiably be attributed to every living creature'.[13] The charm of children, according to Freud,

Arthur Drummond, 'His Majesty the Baby', 1898, engraving.

lies to a great extent in their narcissism, their 'self-contentment and inaccessibility'. Parental love for their children, in turn, is nothing but the parents' narcissism born again. Furthermore, from Freud's conservative and anti-feminist social perspective, women who are good-looking can take narcissistic pleasure in their appearance, as compensation for the social restriction placed on their relationships.[14]

One other crucial point Freud makes about narcissism concerns the development of the 'ego ideal' – an ideal model for the self, against which a person can self-critically measure their own performance. Though this might seem in some ways a negative agency, designed to point out the ego's shortcomings, Freud suggests that it acts as a subtle displacement of a person's original self-love: 'What he projects before him as his ideal is the substitute for the lost narcissism of his childhood in which he was his own ideal.'[15] This disguised or displaced form of self-love provides an important link to Freud's emerging conceptions of social psychology. As will be touched on later in this chapter, traits of the 'ego ideal' can form a common bond for a social group, a class or a nation, just as Freud believed that currents of homosexual desire were rechannelled into friendship, *esprit de corps* and 'the love of mankind in general'.[16]

From having been fairly invisible in the first decade of Freud's work, the new theorization of narcissism made it a crucial element in the bond between parents and children, mothers and babies, same-sex love and group identification, as well as in the analysis of paranoia, auto-eroticism and hypochondria. No wonder that at the end of the 1970s Christopher Lasch's best-selling *The Culture of Narcissism* would draw heavily on Freud and the post-Freudians to launch an assault on American self-absorption, self-indulgence and presentism. But narcissism is also significantly linked to the theme of 'mythologization': if the ego is to a certain extent bound to others and to the world by webs of love and self-love, then the distinction between pleasure and reason, fantasy and reality, is not so clear. Pleasure now left an indelible structural mark, not just on dreams, but on self-consciousness as a whole, such that one might never entirely emerge from myths of one's own making.

Archaic Desires

If the publication of Jung's *Transformations and Symbols of the Libido* and Freud's *Totem and Taboo* was the culmination of a turn to myth, by 1912 that turn had also developed into a territorial and ideological war between the two leaders of the psychoanalytic movement. What had happened to sour the relationship with Jung that, since their first meeting in 1907, had only grown in intensity and intellectual creativity? Their falling-out created a tear not only in the fabric of psychoanalytic theory, but in the constitution of the international movement itself. Though driven by personal factors – including different professional and social milieus and a somewhat equivocal friendship, masking an underlying rivalry – there were also unresolved theoretical differences. Jung, from the start, was unwilling to grant the centrality of sexuality in psychic life in the same way as Freud. Though he conceded that sexual libido had a large part to play in neurotic illnesses, he could not accept that this was sufficient to account for the more radical disturbance of mental life encountered in psychosis.

It seems that up until 1911 the excitement of opening up the new psychology of the unconscious together was enough to sustain the middle ground between them. But there was something about the speculative terrain of mythology that – possibly because it existed at a tangent to clinical work – allowed it to become the site of a radical challenge. What followed during 1911–12 is hard to unravel because the divisions emerged silently, beneath the veneer of Jung's often ingratiating manner towards Freud, and Freud's affable but condescending encouragement. But in Part One of Jung's *Transformations and Symbols*, published in August 1911, he revealed how the immersion in myth and religion was enabling him to formulate other kinds of primary psychological tendencies than the sexual.

In such maps of ancient psychic struggle as myth provided, Jung was finding evidence of a conflict at the heart of sexuality itself, between a more bestial element (Freud's sexual libido) and a force unconsciously compelling the ego towards culture. Freud's response – 'I am delighted by the many points of agreement with things I have already said or would *like* to say'[17] – was near-sighted and inadequate, failing to credit Jung's originality but also missing the extent to which Jung was fashioning a major challenge to the 'sexual' psyche. In correspondence towards the end of 1911 Jung voiced his concerns more directly. He levelled an attack at a weak spot in Freud's account of the Schreber case, notably where Freud had described the catastrophic breakdown between subject and reality in psychosis. If libido was not just *sexual* desire, but underpinned a more general bond between the individual and the outer world, did this not undermine Freud's distinction between a reality principle and a pleasure principle, conscious realism and unconscious wishing? Freud's paper on narcissism, not written until early 1914, was in part an attempt to clear up this ambiguity – in effect, by conceding that the ego was suffused by its own version of sexuality: narcissism. Thus Freud's belated response to Jung's challenge was to make sexuality evermore pervasive in human consciousness. But Jung developed the problem in a different style. He argued that Freud, in blurring the distinction between 'sexual libido' and 'ego libido', had implicitly opened the way for a psychoanalysis grounded in a different reading of libido as a broader, non-sexual, even spiritual tendency embedded in life.

For a moment there followed an uneasy lull – Jung promised a 'new solution' in the forthcoming Part Two of the *Symbols* text. Meanwhile, Freud began to pen his own rival statement on the origins of religion. It was during that same summer of 1912 that Freud, enjoying a 'melancholy solitude' in Rome, visited San Pietro in Vincoli daily to gaze on Michelangelo's sculpture of Moses, admiring how the statue depicted not the breaking of the tablets of law in wrath, but the curbing of that impulse, expressing the highest mental achievement: 'that of [a person] struggling successfully against an inward passion for the sake of a cause to which he has devoted himself'.[18]

The blow came in September with the publication of the second half of Jung's text in which he set out a counter-statement to Freudian theory in no uncertain terms. In *Three Essays on the Theory of Sexuality*, Jung proposed, Freud had conceived of the term 'libido' in the narrow sense of sexual need. But more recently its field of application had been widened. Drawing once more on the Schreber case and the loss of reality function, Jung argued that there must be some other kind of libido, or a non-sexual portion of it, that was involved in such profound psychical transformations. For evidence he gestured towards countless functions in nature that had once formed part of the impulse towards propagation, but which, already at an earlier point in evolutionary history, had been redirected from sexuality to other practical tasks – nest-building in birds, or the protection of young.[19] Where Freudians saw sexual complexes manifesting themselves ubiquitously and unambiguously in ancient mythologies, Jung countered that ever since prehistoric times myth-making and other cultural and religious activities had mobilized 'an already differentiated or desexualized quantity of libido' in the service of the reality function.[20] Libido in its primal form had an endless natural plasticity and should therefore be considered as a general force of desire, or psychical energy – more akin to Arthur Schopenhauer's 'will', or even 'the cosmogenic meaning of Eros in Plato and Hesiod'.[21]

In a second blow, Jung, who was at the time on tour, lecturing at Fordham University in New York, announced publicly that 'there is nothing for it but to abandon the sexual definition of libido,' and he wrote to Freud in November claiming that his new perspective had won over many Americans.[22] This time Freud was clear about the damage done to his theoretical edifice, his tables of law. As he commented drily in his polemical history of the psychoanalytic movement, written a year and a half later: 'For sexual libido an abstract concept has been substituted, of which one may safely say that it remains mystifying and incomprehensible.' Jung and Adler had made the mistake of picking out 'a few cultural overtones from the symphony of life' but had 'failed to hear the mighty and primordial melody of the instincts'.[23]

The break followed not long after in the form of an ill-tempered exchange of letters at the end of 1912. Jung objected violently to Freud's tendency to treat his followers like patients. Freud, in response, depicted Jung comically as one who 'while behaving abnormally keeps shouting that he is normal', and proposed they abandon their personal relationship entirely.[24] Despite the disclaimers each put forward about having relinquished their emotional attachment, the split was immensely painful and destructive. Jung remained formally within the International Psychoanalytic Association for another year – indeed he was still its president – but during 1913 he started to feel increasingly disoriented. He resigned from his academic post in Zürich, lost many of his friends, and not long after the dispiriting fourth psychoanalytic congress in Munich in September, which was the last time he and Freud ever met, Jung found himself in a state of constant tension, beset by visions of bloodshed and European calamity. He finally resigned from the International Psychoanalytic Association in April 1914, shortly before the publication of Freud's damning critique of himself and Adler in 'On the History of the Psychoanalytic Movement'. Out of the fragments of Jung's mental turmoil, his 'confrontation with the unconscious' as he called it, were already emerging the elements of his own mythopoeic system, analytical psychology, which would eventually bring him world renown.

Oedipus Among the 'Savages'

The capstone of these interpersonal and conceptual struggles over the desexualization of the psyche arrived with the completion of *Totem and Taboo* – Freud's vivid, speculative prehistoric narrative that was his final word on Jung's 'libido', and which inaugurated a later phase in Freud's intellectual life, in which his gaze would shift increasingly to the psychosocial. This work – Freud's 'grand synthesis' on the meaning of psychoanalysis and of religion – had been gestating since 1910, its four parts being published in instalments in *Imago* from mid-January 1912 to June 1913, almost in a race with Jung. Drawing various parallels between the behaviour of neurotic subjects and the 'primitive' cultures depicted by Victorian anthropologists such as J. G. Frazer and E. B. Tylor, the premises throughout were thoroughly shaped by colonial and evolutionary geographies. There were 'savages' living at the fringes of civilized empires in Oceania, the East Indies, Africa and Australia who still worshipped totems and who 'we believe, stand very near to primitive man'.[25] Their institutions thus provided insight into the most basic and earliest forms of social organization. At the same time, the psychic life of neurotics – with whom they were being compared – started to be represented as regressive in an evolutionary sense.

If the work is a culmination of that turn towards mythology that maps the basic assumptions of the Freudian unconscious over a much broader socio-cultural terrain, its second task was undoubtedly to quash Jung's 'renegade' version of psychoanalysis by formally stamping the core motifs of Freudian sexual theory at the heart of the most ancient institutions and experiences. These motifs, dealt with in successive essays, were the threat of incest and its repression; love and hostility directed at parents; the libidinization of mental life resulting in 'magical' thinking; and the infant's death wishes against the father. The main points of the text can be formulated quite simply. In the first piece Freud turns to Australia – the youngest continent but, in an egregious reflection of the language of the settlers, home to 'the most backward and miserable of savages'[26] – to explore the system of totemism, which among the Aborigines took the place of religious and social institutions.

What captured Freud's attention in particular was the way in which subservience to the totem (each individual belongs to a totem clan that identifies with a particular totem animal) is accompanied by laws of exogamy: '[in] almost every place where we find totems we also find *a law against persons of the same totem having sexual relations with one another and consequently against their marrying*'.[27] The conclusion Freud draws is that the most 'archaic' communities demonstrate a horror of incest consonant with the sexual anxieties he had posited at the heart of family life, and which he was now referring to as the Oedipus complex. Freud felt he was able to show 'that these same incestuous wishes, which are later destined to become unconscious, are still regarded by savage peoples as immediate perils'.[28]

In the second essay Freud looked at the same phenomena from the angle of 'taboo'. As with the prohibitions adopted by obsessional neurotics, taboos appear to 'have no grounds and are of unknown origin', dating back to a period before the birth of any formal religion.[29] The obsessional patient is aware only of 'an undefined feeling that some particular person in his environment will be injured as a result of the violation'.[30] But the two most ancient and significant taboo prohibitions coincide with the two laws of totemism: 'not to kill the totem animal and to avoid sexual intercourse with members of the totem clan of the opposite sex'.[31] It follows, once again, that these 'must be the oldest and most powerful of human desires', and correspondingly that neurotics – who reproduce similar taboos, but in a more idiosyncratic and individual fashion – 'may be said to have inherited an archaic constitution'.[32]

In the third essay, building on his case histories of the Rat Man and Judge Schreber, Freud links the principles implicit in magical practices – for instance, the belief that individuals can affect each other through rituals performed with mimetic gestures, words or thoughts – to the psychoanalytic notion of 'omnipotent' thinking prevalent in infancy. Here was a general basis for understanding the affectively powerful operation of thoughts and wishes: a magical function, culturally more archaic than any religious belief, and psychologically more primary than any form of conscious judgement. Freud speculated that in 'primitive peoples', just as with modern 'narcissists', 'the process of thinking is still to a great extent sexualized.'[33]

Freud's argument builds to a climax in the fourth essay, 'The Return of Totemism in Childhood'. Beginning with a review of existing theories of animal totems, Freud then presents psychoanalytic clinical material on animal phobias that symbolize death wishes against the father, finally proposing that an original murder of the father lay behind the archaic institution of totems and taboos in primeval history. For neither the first nor the last time in his oeuvre, Freud called on the reader to suspend disbelief while he sketched a mythic narrative that aimed to tie the loose ends of the study together in a single intuition – 'a hypothesis which may seem fantastic but which offers the advantage of establishing an unsuspected correlation between groups of phenomena that have hitherto been disconnected'.[34] Freud drew in part on the researches of the biblical scholar William Robertson Smith, who in his *Religion of the Semites* (1889) postulated that the oldest form of sacrifice was the sacrifice of animals – totem animals – whose flesh was eaten in order to establish a common bond between a god and its worshippers. Freud combined this with a very different source: Darwin's supposition that the earliest state of society was akin to that of gorillas and took the form of a 'primal horde', a small group of females under the dominance of a despotic 'primal father', who repelled intruders and drove out his own male offspring. Freud then invites us to consider how the institutions of totemism, religion and culture might have emerged from an original Oedipal crime – a first sacrifice – within such a communal group:

> One day the brothers who had been driven out came together, killed and devoured their father and so made an end of the patriarchal horde . . . Cannibal savages as they were, it goes without saying that they devoured their victim as well as killing him. The violent primal father had doubtless been the feared and envied model of each one of the company of brothers: and in the act of devouring him they accomplished their identification with him, and each one of them acquired a portion of his strength.[35]

The bloody act, however, produces long-lasting psychical repercussions. After the banished sons had satisfied their hatred of the father, the obstacle to their cravings for power and sexual desire, 'the affection which had all this time been pushed under was bound to make itself felt.'[36] They revoked the deed, from then on forbidding the killing of the totem (a symbolic substitute for the father) and renounced their claim to the women they had liberated. 'They thus created out of their filial sense of guilt the two fundamental taboos of totemism,' which corresponds to the two repressed wishes of the Oedipus complex.[37] Not only did totemic institutions arise from this first experience of guilt – a remorseful, deferred obedience to the murdered father – but Freud believed the echo of this act was transmitted through later forms of religious culture and their sacred feasts: the Christian Eucharist was a 'repetition and a commemoration of this memorable and criminal deed, which was the beginning of so many things – of social organization, of moral restrictions and of religion'.[38]

Like the Dora study, *Totem and Taboo* has never ceased to offer a red rag to its critics – one failure being that, just as ethnographic fieldwork was about to emerge as definitive for the modern discipline of anthropology, Freud was reliant on the speculations of armchair mythographers who based their theories on the reports of primitive customs and superstitions now circulating along the colonial trade routes, which they invested with their own Orientalizing fantasies about the nature of 'savage' or archaic life. The book is thus packed with vignettes of 'otherness' and of curious practices, such as those among the inhabitants of Lepers' Island in the New Hebrides, for whom, when 'a boy knows that certain footprints in the road are his sister's, he will not follow them, nor will she follow his'; or the Gilyak hunter whose children are forbidden to make drawings on wood or sand while he is out hunting; or the widows among the Shuswap from British Columbia, forbidden to touch their own head or body during mourning.[39]

And yet Freud's point is that these procedures are not *other* to us. Past and present shimmer over each 'other' here – the high priest of Jupiter in ancient Rome, whose 'hair could be cut only by a free man and with a bronze knife', resonates with the obsessional wife in twentieth-century Vienna, who banned her husband's razor from the home because it had been bought from a shop next to an undertakers.[40] Such fusions of myth with modernity anticipate much modernist writing of the next decade, including H.D., T. S. Eliot, James Joyce and the French Surrealists. One way of reading *Totem and Taboo* is as, itself, a remarkable piece of modernist literature, which uses the threads of the old world to gather up the fragments of the new.

But the text also created a problematic legacy, especially for a project that aimed at an emancipatory psychology, in that Freud ended up closely weaving his clinical theory of the unconscious and repression with assumptions organized by the colonial paradigm itself. Or at least this implication is brought out far more emphatically by Freud's 'archaic' turn. The notion of the libidinal, and the mentally 'primitive', set against the precarious governorship of the ego, inscribes a repressive political dynamic at the heart of psychic life. In 1915 Freud would compare the content of the unconscious to 'an aboriginal population in the mind'[41] – implying that 'primitive' peoples, like primitive thoughts, require repression in order for a society to function. In the same year he noted that wars between 'the primitive and the civilized peoples, between the races who are divided by the colour of their skin' would occupy mankind for some time to come.[42] Such correlations were carried forward in the assumptions of colonial psychologists and psychiatrists in the 1940s, as they interpreted nationalist uprisings in neurotic terms, as forms of infantilism, or expressions of a 'dependency complex' driven towards insecurity by the weakening of colonial administrations.[43] It was a paradigm that was brilliantly critiqued and dismantled by another psychoanalytic thinker, the psychiatrist and radical advocate of decolonization Frantz Fanon, in the 1950s.

Read ethnographically, *Totem and Taboo* thus presents a very unstable methodological mix of, on the one hand, the vast pretensions of an evolutionary argument, and on the other the incorporation of a highly speculative hypothesis – a 'Just So Story', as he would in part concede. Freud had effectively taken one myth – that of Oedipus – and written it into the core of a new, social evolutionary one. This mirrors Freud's tactics in introducing an argument about phylogenesis to support his hypothesis of a primal scene, as mentioned earlier in relation to the Wolf Man. That text was drafted in the winter of 1914–15 and, like *Totem and Taboo*, attempted the description of 'deep strata of mental life' never before attacked.[44] With such works Freud attempted to seal off the alternative futures for psychoanalysis pursued by Adler and Jung, setting the twin features of the Oedipus complex (infantile sexuality and death wishes against the father) into the prehistoric past of humanity, as an indelible feature of the mind. But it was precisely this attempt at establishing the Oedipus complex on a universal footing – bringing psychology, biology and anthropology into a single frame of reference – that would prove the Achilles heel of Freud's anthropological project, and it was quickly subject to critiques from new researchers who instead emphasized the functional description of living communities and variable cultural patterns.

Two of the earliest leaders in modern anthropology – Bronisław Malinowski in Britain and Margaret Mead in America – used their studies in the 1920s (of sexual life in the Trobriand Islands, and coming of age in Samoa) to challenge Freud's hypotheses. Malinowski felt he had proved that there was no repression of infantile sexuality in Melanesia, and Mead that children growing up in larger communal groups in Samoa failed to develop an Oedipus complex. Still, both critics felt that Freud *had* identified a 'nuclear complex' applicable to Western patriarchal society, and when Freud posited, at the end of *Totem and Taboo*, that the problems of social psychology would prove soluble 'on the basis of one single concrete point – man's relation to his father'[45] he forecast not only some of his own later concerns, but a thesis that had a large amount of traction in mid-century social science, from the cultural anthropology of Mead and Ruth Benedict, to the sociology of Theodor Adorno and Talcott Parsons. Freud's thesis about the savagery that lay just beneath the veneer of European culture would also prove timely for a world about to endure the most catastrophic conflict, one that would bring about the collapse of the world Freud had grown up in.

Europe 1914–18: The Imperishable Primitive

The assassination of Archduke Franz Ferdinand in June 1914, and the declarations of war that followed, caught Freud by surprise, and it took him several months to find his bearings. In spring 1915

Sigmund Freud with his sons Ernst and Martin, 1916.

he gave public voice to feelings of disorientation and protested the way in which censorship reduced citizens to the level of children, forced to sanction the State's lust for power.[46] But in the immediate summer and autumn of 1914 Freud was caught up in patriotic enthusiasm, announcing to colleagues that he now felt himself an Austrian, and expected a speedy victory for the German people. According to Ernest Jones, 'He was excitable, irritable, and made slips of the tongue all day long.'[47] His sons all served, as well as many of his psychoanalytic colleagues: Ferenczi as a medical officer with the Hungarian Hussars; Abraham in a military hospital outside Berlin, and then with the navy in Eastern Prussia.

The psychoanalytic movement had now fragmented. The congress planned for September was cancelled, journals were suspended and Freud's clinical practice was greatly reduced. Having previously seen about ten patients a day, he was down to only two analysands by October 1914. Freud complained to Ernest Jones that 'What Jung and Adler have left of the movement is now perishing in the strife of nations.'[48] Such gloomier thoughts were gathered into a set of reflections written in March and April 1915, in which Freud addressed the feeling of shock experienced when civilized society plunged into a war 'more bloody and more destructive' than any other.[49] But in an unexpected twist, which drew on the thesis formulated in *Totem and Taboo*, he argued that the apparent destruction of so much that is precious was itself an illusion. Beneath high European culture lay archaic instincts waiting for the opportunity to break out, for 'the primitive mind is . . . imperishable'.[50] Conscience proved to be superficial, merely a form of social anxiety. Judged by unconscious wishful impulses, Freud added, 'we ourselves are, like primaeval man, a gang of murderers.'[51]

Despite the dire prognosis, it turned out to be significant that Freud had fought his own wars already in 1912–14. The triptych *Totem and Taboo*, 'On Narcissism' and 'On the History of the

Sigmund Freud with his inner circle of supporters, Berlin congress 1922. Standing, left to right: Otto Rank, Karl Abraham, Max Eitingon, Ernest Jones. Sitting, left to right: Freud, Sándor Ferenczi, Hanns Sachs.

Psycho-analytic Movement' had to a certain extent won the bid, within the movement, to retain the distinctiveness of Freud's vision on his own terms. As he put it bluntly at the opening of his historical account: 'I consider myself justified in maintaining that even today no one can know better than I do what psychoanalysis is.'[52] To aid Freud in the task of defending this psychoanalysis, Jones had in 1912 mooted a 'Secret Committee' of Freudian loyalists – to include Ferenczi, Rank, Abraham and Jones himself – who in the wake of Adler and then Jung's defections were to 'guard the kingdom and policy of their master'. The committee had met for the first time in May 1913, and to seal the bond each member was given an antique Greek intaglio from Freud's collection, which they set into gold rings. The resilience of the movement thus re-founded would become clearer by the end of the decade. But what transpired during the period 1914–16 was a different kind of flourishing. Left to his own devices by the drastic reduction in clinical hours,

Freud was freed up for new writing projects, updating and modifying some core psychoanalytic concepts and developing new articulations of therapeutic practice.

On this latter front, in the summer of 1914, Freud added to a series of short papers he had been writing since 1911 on aspects of clinical technique. Some of the observations on technique Freud had made during 1911–13 included a move away from extended dream interpretations to focus on what the patient brought to any particular session, and the recommendation that the doctor should put aside feelings, even sympathy, and aim at opacity, turning their unconscious 'like a receptive organ towards the transmitting unconscious of the patient'.[53] Another shift was that psychoanalysis was now to focus more decidedly on generating the 'transference' (discussed earlier in the Dora case), the unconscious re-experiencing, in the analytic session, of attachment relationships from the infantile past which are 'transferred' unwittingly onto the therapist, raising questions (evermore so in modern psychotherapeutic practice) over *who* the analyst is for the patient at any one moment in a clinical session. In 1914 Freud drafted some important additions to this literature on transference, in which he described how patients are compelled to repeat, rather than remember, their illness. The move from unconscious to conscious knowledge was now to be accomplished via a gradual, controlled re-emergence and working-through of infantile desires and aggressions, a halfway house between fantasy and reality.

On a more public footing, Freud also delivered three sets of 'Introductory Lectures' in the winter semesters of 1915–16 and 1916–17 at the University of Vienna. Much as the talks at Clark University, these gave a basic exposition of the psychoanalytic point of view on slips and bungled actions, moving onto dreams, and ending with the meaning of neurosis. They have little to offer in the way of new insights, but were long treated as an accessible introductory guide to psychoanalytic thinking and were translated into fourteen languages in Freud's lifetime. But by far the most significant product of the war years was a sequence of papers investigating the basic terms of psychoanalytic theory, such as drive, repression and the unconscious. Psychical processes are here revisited from a number of different perspectives, which Freud now termed 'metapsychological'. The 'economic' aspect deals with psychology in terms of notional quantities of energy, needing to be bound, displaced or released through action; the 'topographic' approach renders the psyche as a set of differentiated parts, functioning as a system, while the 'dynamic' view pays attention to internal conflict. Freud also revised many of his assumptions, often quite substantially, in the light of new developments such as the theory of narcissism.

There is no space to go into the details of these papers here. 'Instincts and Their Vicissitudes' traces how drives can be transformed or redirected in several different ways; 'The Unconscious' consolidates a new perception that the unconscious covers more than simply the 'repressed' – important functions of the ego (the repressing agent) are also unconscious. What is striking about these essays is the way in which Freud declined to produce any systematic overview. In July 1915 he wrote to his friend and psychoanalytic colleague Lou Andreas-Salomé that he had finished a draft of a 'metapsychology book' containing twelve essays.[54] However, seven of these were abandoned or destroyed, and in further wartime letters to Andreas-Salomé he defended his model of working 'without the inner need for completion', renouncing cohesion and harmony.[55] Though they have retained their significance for clinicians and academics to this day, these metapsychological papers were also interim products – part of a process of internal renegotiation that would eventually come to fruition in a more dramatic trilogy of publications following the end of the war.

Before exploring these late revisions, it remains to take stock of the collapse of the Austro-Hungarian and German empires – for which, by the end of the conflict, Freud professed to weep not a single tear.[56] The armistice signed by both nations in November 1918 inaugurated a gradual dissolution of their component parts, including, for the Austrians, the sundering of the dual monarchy with Hungary and the loss of Moravia (Freud's birthplace), as well as the polyglot regions whose discourse had threaded through Freud's adult dreams. In the reminiscence of Stefan Zweig, 'Czechs, Poles, Italians and Slovenians had taken back their lands, leaving a mutilated torso bleeding from all its arteries.'[57] The 'Red' Vienna of the Social Democrats was born, and republics were declared in Weimar and Bavaria. Hungary – which Freud had hoped could develop into a second capital for the movement under the management of Ferenczi – was now particularly unstable, witnessing the rise first of Bela Kun's short-lived communist regime, followed by a White Terror.

In these years of extreme political and financial instability, poverty and hunger, the Freud family gradually reassembled itself – Martha survived pneumonia in the spring of 1919, and their sons returned from the war (Martin was held captive in Italy until the end of the year). Since 1917 they had endured food shortages and terrible winters, and there was the further loss of all their savings as the Austrian currency plummeted, though American and English relatives stepped in to help with money and food parcels. The biggest blow of all came in January 1920, when Freud's favourite daughter, Sophie Halberstadt, pregnant with her third child, fell ill with influenza and died within a few days. Just three years later, in June 1923, he would endure an even harder loss, that of Sophie's youngest son, Heinele, then four and a half. Freud was aware 'of never having loved a human being, certainly never a child, so much',[58] and Jones notes that this was the only occasion on which Freud was known to cry.

But there were also signs of hope at the beginning of the 1920s. One was a new link Freud forged to the future of psychoanalysis, through his youngest daughter. Anna Freud, the last child to be left at home, had begun to discuss her dreams with Freud in 1915 and attended his 'Introductory Lectures' a year later. In October 1918, in part to deal with indecision over her career as a teacher, but also perhaps to resolve her 'father complex', she went into analysis with him, six days a week, with some interruption, until the spring of 1922, and again briefly in 1924–5 – a fact not widely known at the time, which, though it appears controversial in light of the development of psychoanalytic professional ethics, had precedents in early psychoanalytic circles. Anna Freud accompanied her father triumphantly to the first post-war international congress, held in The Hague in 1920, and during the following decade applied psychoanalytic educational methods in schools in Vienna, as well as pioneering the psychoanalysis of children. After 1922 she would substitute for Freud's presence at the annual congresses, and soon began to make her own definitive contributions to the future of psychoanalytic theory.

Sigmund and Anna Freud at the Hague congress, 1920.

On the broader international scale psychoanalysis experienced a marvellous resurgence, due in part to experimentation with psychoanalytic techniques as a treatment for shell-shocked soldiers in parts of Europe towards the end of the war: for instance by the German Ernst Simmel, who treated numerous trauma cases in a field hospital in Posen; or by W.H.R. Rivers working with shell-shocked patients at Craiglockhart Hospital, near Edinburgh. According to Rivers,

> It is a wonderful turn of fate that just as Freud's theory of the unconscious and the method of psychoanalysis founded upon it should be so hotly discussed, there should have occurred events which have produced on an enormous scale just those conditions of paralysis, contracture, phobia and obsession, which the theory was especially designed to explain.[59]

Other signs of post-war renewal included the 1920 launch of the *International Journal of Psychoanalysis*, and Freud's clinical practice picked up – in particular he began to receive foreign patients from the United States and Britain, bringing much-needed harder currency. Some of these were now coming not so much for treatment as for supervision in order to become analysts themselves. Such were the Americans Abram Kardiner and Ruth Mack Brunswick, and from Britain, John Rickman and Joan Riviere, and the Bloomsbury couple Alix and James Strachey (future editor of 'The Standard Edition' of Freud's collected works in English). The latter pair arrived in Vienna a few months after their marriage in June 1920. Once in analysis James reported to his brother Lytton: 'As for what it's all about, I'm vaguer than ever; but at all events it's sometimes extremely exciting and sometimes extremely unpleasant – so I daresay there's *something* in it.'[60]

Vienna after the war was not the centre of psychoanalysis but the hub of a widening circle of branch societies in other countries, which were now translating and popularizing Freud's work and developing their own psychoanalytic institutions. The most important of these were in London, New York and Berlin, where a 'Poliklinik' was founded in February 1920, answering Freud's call for psychoanalysts to pioneer large-scale applications of therapy, because 'neuroses threaten public health no less than tuberculosis.'[61] A number of analysts gravitated here from Hungary and Austria, contributing to a formal teaching institute that was opened in 1923. But psychoanalytic societies were growing much further afield: in Calcutta, where a Bengali doctor, Girindrasekhar Bose, inaugurated the Indian Psychoanalytic Society in 1922; and in the same year a society and institute were set up in Moscow and in Kazan on the Volga. Psychoanalysis, at least until 1923, was flourishing in post-revolutionary Russia. According to Jones, Jewish immigrants were even arriving in Palestine from Galicia 'with no clothes, but with a copy of *Das Kapital* and *Die Traumdeutung* under their arms'.[62]

A New Mythology for a New Psychology

It was in this vibrant context that Freud introduced his most important theoretical statements since *The Interpretation of Dreams* and *Three Essays:* a trilogy of texts – *Beyond the Pleasure Principle* (1920), *Group Psychology* (1921) and *The Ego and the Id* (1923) – which represented the culmination of many of the ideas trialled in the papers on metapsychology, but now more fully worked through and coherently integrated. Together they inaugurate a late phase of Freud's work, which is sufficiently different in emphasis from that of the early 1900s to warrant being called a 'second model', or reformulation of psychoanalytic theory. Three things stand out about these more comprehensive texts, besides the surge in intellectual productivity. One is the degree to which Freud was stepping beyond the bounds of individual psychology. Each of these texts, in different ways, places the individual in a wider context of the formation and disintegration of communities, at various social, biological and historical levels.

A second point is the shift of focus from the unconscious to the ego, which was now not only the seat of reality testing and censorship, but could be impoverished (in melancholia), or invested with libido. It was also subject to an 'ego ideal' and the critical agency of conscience, and bore the trace of former object relations. Research had so far directed the interest of psychoanalysis too exclusively to the repressed, Freud would write: 'We should like to learn more about the ego, now that we know that it, too, can be unconscious.'[63] There was also something more holistic about Freud's later approach to the psyche – a thing of many different parts and relationships, besides the original split-off ideas, dreams or symptoms. Put simply, more of everyday mental life gets in: jealousy, mourning, guilt, morality, judgement, abstract ideals and uncanny experiences (in 1925 he would comment on the ego functions of walking, eating and professional work).

Directly related to this last point, there is a third: an increased focus on human aggression, which takes up a much more prominent position alongside sexuality. This fuller elaboration of the hostile components in human behaviour had built up over the course of a few shorter wartime texts. It is there emphatically in 'Instincts and Their Vicissitudes', where Freud underlines the ways in which the ego 'abhors and pursues with intent to destroy all objects which are a source of unpleasurable feeling for it'.[64] Other shorter texts dealt with children's sado-masochistic fantasies of beatings, and with horror fiction. One of the most interesting developments along these lines was in another metapsychological paper, 'Mourning and Melancholia' – a text devoted not so much to grief as to narcissistic aggressivity, which Freud was beginning to develop into a theory of the origins of conscience. He focused here on the way depression finds utterance in self-reproaches, culminating in a 'delusional expectation of punishment', and derives these from a hatred, originally directed towards an external object of attachment but now turned back upon the subject.[65]

Many of these concerns come to the fore in *Beyond the Pleasure Principle*, one of Freud's most fascinating but also intractably puzzling texts, which provoked immediate opposition in Freud's inner circle, as well as proving enduringly divisive within the psychoanalytic movement. Psychoanalysis had always presumed that mental events are automatically governed by a pleasure principle that experiences increases in tension as unpleasurable, and therefore seeks to diminish the quantity of excitement impinging on the psychical apparatus, whether from external sources or internal ones, such as sexuality. However, a number of problems had started to disturb this paradigm. One was the experience of soldiers suffering from war neurosis who were plagued by repetitive anxiety dreams. What possible pleasure could this serve? Freud elucidates this via an observation he had made of Sophie's elder child, Ernst, when he was one-and-a-half. Ernst occupied himself by throwing his toys away from him, while expressing his satisfaction through a long-drawn-out 'o-o-o-o', which Freud and Sophie interpreted as '*fort*' or 'gone'. The child was evidently symbolizing the periodic disappearance of his mother (as a year later he would symbolize the absence of his father by punishing his toys with a 'Go to the fwont!').[66] But why would the child constantly replay the departure of his parents, which couldn't have been experienced as pleasure? Freud supposes that the child could be satisfying a repressed impulse for revenge, or trying to master an overpowering passive experience by repeating it as an active one.

It seems a marginal point, about the satisfactions or comforts of repetition, but in Freud's masterfully layered text it will lead from the infant's cot all the way back to the origins of organic life. The guiding thread is what Freud terms the 'compulsion to repeat', which he links to the clinical transference – patients' propensity to re-experience phenomena from infancy. Such repetitions involve not just buried infantile wishes, but also experiences that could never originally have been pleasurable, such as the loss of love, or a permanent injury to self-regard. This strand of enquiry leads to the radical heart of the text – a reassessment of the nature of the drive per se, which, according to Freud, demonstrates such a compulsion to repeat, 'more primitive, more elementary, more instinctual than the pleasure principle which it over-rides'.[67]

It is here that Freud allows himself to go down an entirely new pathway for psychoanalysis – albeit one that he himself qualifies as 'often far-fetched speculation'. The crux of the argument turns on a second vignette – not little Ernst, but a model of the basic unit of life as a 'little fragment of living substance' suspended in a world charged 'with the most powerful energies', which would annihilate it were it not provided with a protective shield against excessive stimulation.[68] Although Freud's reference is to protists and protozoa, the image was eloquently mobilized by the German cultural theorist Walter Benjamin in 1936 to depict the shock of war for a generation that had 'gone to school on a horse-drawn streetcar' but grew up to find themselves exposed 'in a field of force of destructive torrents and explosions', as a 'tiny, fragile human body'.[69] Freud proposes that when the protective shield is breached, the unit of life must attempt to master the excess stimulus that has flooded its interior. The new model Freud constructs on this basis conceives of the drive as '*an urge inherent in organic life to restore an earlier state of things*' which had been abandoned under external pressure.[70] Drives are by nature conservative, with the original being the drive 'to return to the inanimate state'.[71] Freud notoriously terms this 'the death drive'.

What so unsettled psychoanalysts at the time was how starkly this overturned Freud's earlier model. Where formerly the major divide in instinctual life had been between the self-preservative drive of the ego and the sexual drives (which needed to undergo repression for the ego to survive), now the over-arching opposition was between the life drives ('the Eros of the poets and philosophers'[72]), which combine the forces of libido with those of the ego, and the death drive. Whereas the forces of Eros are relatively vocal in human life, those of death work silently, but might be inferred as being somehow involved in phenomena such as masochism, in the destructive qualities of conscience, or in patients' 'negative therapeutic reactions' to the treatment.

Much ink has been spilled attempting to correlate this major shift with the experience of war. Surely, critics have argued, it was the scenes of carnage exposed on the battlefields of Europe that forced a 'death drive' unexpectedly onto Freud's theoretical agenda? Others have supposed that it was a belated recognition of anxieties over the ageing process, or a way of grieving the impact of Sophie's death – an assertion which, even at the time, Freud stepped in to contradict by pointing out that the bulk of the text had been drafted the year before her illness. Peter Gay and Ernest Jones raise the interesting possibility that Freud was so late in foregrounding aggression in his work simply because this had been the concept championed by Adler, in opposition to Freud's insistent focus on sexuality.[73] But all these suppositions miss the way in which what Freud seems to be trying to account for is not so much death and destruction, although the new model did now give latitude for theorizing a destructive impulse (something spectacularly developed by the child analyst Melanie Klein, first based in Berlin and then London during the 1920s, whose infant patients were invested with the most terrifying internal fantasies). Rather, the problem that Freud was struggling to resolve was something more clinical – the invisible factors working against recovery, which were keeping patients incomprehensibly bound to forms of suffering, or trapped by an inertia that, before now, Freud had no way of theoretically explaining.

What the focus on the 'death drive' in accounts of the text leaves out, though, is the other half of this new equation: the positive valuation of Eros as a force that combines 'organic substances into ever larger unities', and holds living things together. At the human level this is expressed in love and sexuality as an interpersonal tie, and in sublimated form in the binding of groups, societies and nations. In 'Thoughts for the Times on War and Death' (1915), Freud had been anguished not just by the bloody destruction of life, but equally, or perhaps more so, by the interruption of ethical ties 'between the collective individuals of mankind'.[74] It seems that here is to be found Freud's response to the war – not so much in the proposal of the 'death' drive, but in its compensatory opposite, something that in its combination of the self-preservative and the sexual effectively infuses the presupposition of warring, self-serving individuals (so deeply ingrained in a certain strand of conservative political philosophy) with love and sexuality as a force of living connection. In the war essay of 1915, the influence of civilization facilitates an 'ever-increasing transformation of egoistic trends into altruistic and social ones' through the admixture of erotic components.

Despite editor James Strachey's disclaimer that there is little direct connection between *Beyond the Pleasure Principle* and *Group Psychology* (or more properly 'Mass Psychology'), published a year later, the latter text is in fact a daring development of the thesis that 'Eros' is *the* principle that binds individuals into larger units, and which therefore also lifts individual psychology onto the plane of social psychology. Gustave Le Bon's hugely popular 1895 work *The Crowd*, which Freud uses as a reference point throughout, proposed a similar bridge between psychology and biology: 'The psychological group is a provisional being formed of heterogeneous elements, which for a moment are combined, exactly as the cells which constitute a living body.'[75] Freud poses a further question: what is the actual power that unites human individuals into such groups? He once more suggests that the glue is supplied by libido – the 'emotionality' animating not only 'self-love' but 'love for parents and children, friendship and love for humanity in general'.[76]

It is significant that the two forms of social collectivity Freud chooses as a focus in this work are the army and the Christian Church: the former links the paper again to the recent experience of war, and the latter renews the assault on religion begun in *Totem and Taboo*. Freud's point was to expose the way in which both groups, so different in their martial and spiritual functions, are constituted according to the same mechanisms, which can be read in terms of the secular psychology of love. Each, Freud argues, is held together somewhat along the lines of the Oedipal family, by a charismatic attraction to an authority figure, and a sublimated homosocial tie among siblings (as with the band of brothers posited at the foundation of culture in *Totem and Taboo*). Both groups depend on the 'illusion' of a head – Christ, or the army's commander-in-chief – who loves all the individuals in the group equally.[77] Believers are thus made into 'brothers in Christ', and soldiers are comrades-in-arms. If this illusion of love were to be dispelled, both Church and army would dissolve. Freud goes so far as to suggest that it was the unloving brand of Prussian militarism which contributed to the German defeat;[78] if the love of the 'father' is removed, the group may disintegrate in panic or flight.

The Oedipal family is one tie linking the theory of groups to individual psychology; another is the assumption of a 'hypnotic' factor. According to Le Bon, the person in the crowd easily relinquishes the functions of the ego, entering an impressionable automatic state, much like the individual in the hands of a hypnotist, and is prone to mimic others – gestures spread through the group by virtue of contagion. Freud's task was to transplant this analysis, so redolent of the pre-psychoanalytic phase of hypnotic research, into a more contemporary register of sublimated sexual feelings, object-love and identification. For Freud, what lies behind the phenomenon of hypnotic submission is a libidinal tie, which even under normal circumstances inclines the lover to relinquish their will to the beloved, encouraging subjection or compliance. Love, for Freud, is the only factor capable of limiting the individual's originally narcissistic constitution. In the case of hypnosis or groups, a person's narcissistic libido 'overflows' onto the object, which substitutes for an unattained ego ideal of their own, satisfying a dimension of their self-love.

Aspects of Freud's model may at first glance seem lurid or fantastical. For instance, his dependence on Le Bon's psychology of the volatile and dangerous crowd – itself shaped in response to late nineteenth-century political upheaval, including the Paris Commune and the Dreyfus affair – foregrounds an 'unconscious substratum' of the mind imbued with phylogenetic racial characteristics. According to Le Bon, the individual in the crowd is liable to be usurped by the 'spontaneity, the violence, the ferocity

The mysterious Caligari from *The Cabinet of Dr Caligari* (1920, dir. Robert Wiene).

. . . of primitive beings'.[79] Freud, in like manner, readily connects the contemporary crowd with the primeval one conjured in *Totem and Taboo*: 'the primal horde may arise once more out of any random collection.'[80] And yet, he extracted from Le Bon (and other contemporary texts, such as Wilfred Trotter on the 'herd instinct') a set of principles for understanding the way power and authority assert themselves socially and politically, and often irrationally, which resonated throughout the 1920s and '30s. The hypnotic and criminal mastermind was soon to feature in popular culture, for instance in German expressionist films such as *The Cabinet of Dr Caligari* and the *Dr Mabuse* series, and was readily associated with the rise of fascist dictators; critical theorist Theodor Adorno drew directly on Freud's account in his own characterization of the Nazi crowd. But the analysis is just as relevant today, amid twenty-first-century fears of demagoguery, incipient or actual fascism, and the narcissism of political leaders. In Freud's text the social mass is credulous, gravitates towards extreme positions and has no desire or tolerance for the truth: 'They constantly give what is unreal precedence over what is real.'[81] The leader cannot act democratically but must appear capable of violence, loving no one but themselves: they must be of a 'masterful nature, absolutely narcissistic, self-confident and independent.' Thus is awakened the idea of a 'paramount and dangerous personality, towards whom only a passive-masochistic attitude is possible'.[82]

The third of these post-war landmark texts – *The Ego and the Id* (1923) – attempts to pull together the growing number of new observations about the structure of the psyche that had arisen from clinical and theoretical insights over the previous eight years or so. First among these was the recognition that the division between 'conscious' and 'unconscious' was no longer structurally adequate as a basis for theorizing the operations of the psyche. Not only were there many different ways in which psychic material could be unconscious (only some of which coincided with the 'dynamically' repressed material that psychoanalysts were interested in), but the ego itself was only partly affiliated with consciousness. Freud therefore reconfigured the portrait of the mental apparatus around a new axis: not the conscious and the unconscious, but the ego and what he now termed the 'id' – literally the 'it' (German '*Es*'), a term he borrowed from a new psychoanalytic follower, a maverick German physician with an interest in psychosomatic ailments called Georg Groddeck, who used it to represent the way in which people are passively lived by 'unknown and uncontrollable forces'.[83] Rather than just being a repository for repressed ideas, the id is now more clearly the seat of the instincts, or drives – whether libidinal or aggressive – which struggle to force their way through to consciousness. Far more than previous iterations of the unconscious, the id carries with it a sense of the dangerousness of archaic life, representing deeper layers of phylogenetic history.

The 'ego' for its part is also essentially revised from the earlier sense of being the rational voice of consciousness. Freud, for instance, reminds us that the ego 'is first and foremost a bodily ego' – that is, standing for the physical unit of the individual, controlling its motility and projecting its identity in relation to the surfaces and boundaries of the body. It emerges from the id only gradually, under the pressure of social contact and language, and is therefore not sharply separated from it. Such descriptions replace the clarity of the distinction between conscious and unconscious with something far more ambiguous and amorphous. In addition Freud restates the idea, already suggested in 'Mourning and Melancholia', that when a person gives up an object of sexual attachment, as in the childhood Oedipal drama, this causes an alteration in the ego whereby the lost object is set up inside. This may be the 'sole condition' under which the id is able to relinquish its objects. The ego is thus 'a precipitate of abandoned object-cathexes'; it grows in structure and complexity, but at the cost of acquiescing to a certain extent in the id's demands.

A profound instance of such an internal acquisition is what Freud had begun to elaborate in his recent work as the 'ego ideal', but now developed into a more complexly delineated entity in its own right, 'the superego' (*das Über-Ich*, literally, the 'over-I') – behind which 'there lies hidden an individual's first and most important identification', the identification with the father in infancy.[84] This internalized voice of authority enables a child to move on from its Oedipus complex, precisely by *identifying* with and reproducing internally – in the form of a conscience – what had been a confrontation with external authority. In a further twist, this internalized moral agency reaches deep into the id, and has abundant links with the archaic heritage of humankind. Though a moral sense would seem to be a higher social development, the way in which this has been formed, as a precipitate of the abandoned 'father complex', is peculiarly passionate and *irrational*. The 'superego' is therefore particularly prone to get out of hand – to confront the ego with a punitive and unconscious sense of guilt, expressing in disguised form some of the most powerful negative impulses of the id. In obsessional neurosis and depression, it is prone to rage against the ego with particular cruelty, Freud noted. His explanation is that the superego has in such severe cases absorbed instinctual forces from the death drive, which 'often enough succeeds in driving the ego into death'.[85]

The most striking thing in this new model, besides the incorporation of the 'death drive', is the dislodging of the ego from a position of internal authority and veracity. Though Freud would qualify this presentation a little in later texts, there is no doubt that it was intended as a blow to existing accounts of human consciousness (whether spiritual, philosophical or psychological). Something of this position was anticipated in 1917 when, in a short text discussing the resistances people have to accepting psychoanalysis as a science, Freud elaborated on how psychoanalysis has produced a 'third blow' to human self-esteem,

Sigmund Freud, 1922.

following those delivered by Copernicus (the Earth is no longer the centre of the universe) and Darwin (man is not superior to other animals). Freud's contribution is that the ego itself '*is not master in its own house*'[86] – effectively, consciousness is not what it seems, and the ego is but an intermediary, helplessly caught between three masters: the external world, the murderous id and a punishing conscience. Twisting this way and that to please all parties, it clothes unconscious commands with more acceptable conscious rationalizations, disguising the nature of its conflicts and 'only too often yields to the temptation to become sycophantic, opportunist and lying, like a politician who sees the truth but wants to keep his place in popular favour'.[87]

This is the final – perhaps the most far-reaching – rationale for thinking of Freud's later work under the heading of 'mythology'. Not because he drew so heavily on classical myths, or interested himself in delusion, or in the archaic prehistory of culture, nor even because of the speculative model of the drives he himself referred to as a 'mythology'. Rather, it is that he exposes the function of the ego as in some ways intrinsically 'mythologizing', precisely where it appears to organize a coherent truth about itself. It is the ego's function to ward off from awareness the way in which we are always falling apart (until things actually fall apart, that is). What it is that is falling apart is the many facets of internal reality that we are keen to disown or disavow because they do not fit in with what we want to see: coherence, harmony, authority, pleasure, self-love, success, truthfulness. The 'I' functions to layer and transform, managing and mythologizing its interactions with people and with meaning, according to the intensities it can bear, and according to the patterns for channelling tension laid down in childhood, while (ideally) retaining just enough contact with reality to survive in society.

6

Heresies, 1924–39 and After

'But I am cross. I am cross with mankind.'[1]

'Is there such a thing as a natural end to an analysis?' mused Freud in a late clinical paper of 1937, 'Analysis Terminable and Interminable', one of the last such pieces to be published in his lifetime.[2] It marks the distance from the early 1920s, the time of the founding of training institutes and free clinics, and of the optimism of some of Freud's colleagues over new clinical experiments, including Ferenczi's 'active technique' and Otto Rank's belief that analysis need only delve back to an original separation trauma at birth in order to dispose of neuroses once and for all. Though Freud had recognized the expediency of such initiatives, designed to 'adapt the tempo of analytic therapy to the haste of American life',[3] he preferred in this late work to foreground a more cautious and sceptical view: the processes are complex, changes undergone in analysis are often partial or incomplete, gains can be reversed, new traumas emerge under new pressures. Above all, there are the resistances that defend the patient by every possible means against recovery: expressions of unconscious guilt ultimately tied to that power Freud defined as destructiveness, and traced back 'to the original death instinct of living matter'.[4] Analytic treatments can take years, he had acknowledged a decade earlier, and 'magic that is so slow loses its miraculous character'.[5] With such deprecatory gestures, 'Analysis Terminable and Interminable' poses the

Sigmund Freud, 1939.

question not only of when an 'analysis' is finished, but when
psychoanalysis itself would be finished. Moreover, would it be
finished when Freud exited the stage? This is also a question about
the 'natural end' to this present narrative.

Dark Severity

One such limit is provided by Freud's cancer, the illness from
which he died. The first sign of it became noticeable in 1917 as
a disagreeable swelling in his palate. By the spring of 1923 the

swelling required surgery, and the operation revealed a possible malignant growth – a fact that was withheld from Freud so that he could enjoy a final summer trip to Rome with his daughter Anna (newly qualified as a member of the Vienna Psychoanalytic Society). Immediately after, further emergency operations were scheduled to take out portions of his upper jaw and palate on his right side, replacing them with the first of a series of uncomfortable prostheses. Freud was given only five years to live, but in fact survived for another sixteen, during which he underwent as many as thirty further minor operations. After one, just prior to his 75th birthday, he complained to his friend, the writer Arnold Zweig, that he was a shadow of his former self.

Though he continued to offer the 'talking cure' to multiple patients right up to his final months, the surgical interventions damaged his hearing and impeded his speech. In addition, he was beset by palpitations (requiring him intermittently to give up his beloved cigars), and frequent bouts of intense pain, for which he characteristically refused drugs. All of this might account for the the fact that the last fifteen years of Freud's life were marked by a certain severe style. The Austrian novelist Stefan Zweig remarked on a 'harsh and unconditionally militant' quality emerging in his appearance, settling, by 1937, into a 'dark severity'.[6] Leonard Woolf's impression in 1938 was of something 'sombre, suppressed, reserved', like a 'half-extinct volcano'.[7]

The difficult and drawn-out physical ending was at the same time entangled with a set of global and local catastrophes, through which Freud witnessed the gradual collapse of European culture and the moral certainties that had provided the underpinning for his intellectual project, and with it the psychoanalytic institutions in which he had invested his life. 'Analysis Terminable and Interminable' registers in passing the stock market collapse of October 1929, which inaugurated the Great Depression (Otto Rank's experiments with shorter treatments 'are now things of the past – no less than American "prosperity" itself').[8] In the laconic journal, composed of two- or three-word diary entries, begun soon after the collapse under the heading 'Shortest Chronicle', he recorded the modulations of his illness – neuralgia, 'bad heart days', gastric attacks, nosebleeds – but also inserted dramatic political events alongside family birthdays and notable deaths (Sándor Ferenczi, Eugen Bleuler, Arthur Schnitzler) and notices of the latest additions to his antiquities collection. 'Consultation with Pichler' (Freud's oral surgeon) on 14 April 1931 is followed next day by 'Republic in Spain'. February 1933 yields the following surrealistic sequence: 'Iron Buddha' (an acquisition), 'Czech Leonardo' (translation of Freud's 1910 'case study' of the artist) and 'Berlin Parliament on Fire' – a set of historical free associations, but also a stark reminder that the decade in which Freud published his last works was also the decade in which the Nazis began burning them.[9]

Within three years of Freud being awarded the Goethe Prize by the city of Frankfurt, so cherished a goal for someone whose intellect was closely identified with the German language, Hitler had become German Chancellor and Freud's books (for their 'soul-destroying overestimation of the sex life') – along with those of Marx, Einstein, Kafka and hundreds of other Jewish or supposedly dissident and degenerate authors – were cheered onto the pyre flaming before the Berlin Opera House. Freud's sons fled the country – Oliver to France, Ernst (father of Lucian, the artist, and Clement Freud, the broadcaster) to England – while the Jewish psychoanalysts who had run the flagship training institute and clinic in Berlin or spearheaded therapeutic initiatives in other cities (Max Eitingon, Otto Fenichel, Erich Fromm, Edith Jacobsen, Margaret Mahler and countless others) fled the country to England, Norway, the United States, Palestine, South America and elsewhere, thus inaugurating the trauma history of the psychoanalytic movement itself.

'The world is turning into an enormous prison,' Freud wrote in 1933 to Princess Marie Bonaparte, founding member of the

Paris Psychoanalytic Society and one of Freud's key supporters and benefactors in the final years,[10] and to Ernest Jones that same summer he grieved over the perishing of 'our organization': 'Berlin is lost, Budapest devalued through the loss of Ferenczi; where they are heading in America is uncertain.'[11] The purging of the German-speaking psychotherapy world had been swift and carried with it a particular sting, since Carl Jung stepped in to lead a new Nazi-conformed international association that had replaced the German-umbrella Society for Psychotherapy. Jung wasted no time in celebrating the demise of what he – echoing the current antisemitic labels – termed Freud's 'Jewish' medical psychology. Freud, he asserted in an editorial for the society's new organ, 'did not know the Germanic soul'. The 'Aryan unconscious', now emerging, contained 'explosive forces and seeds of a future yet to be born'.[12]

During all this time Freud resisted calls from his closest colleagues to abandon Vienna, worried that this would signal the collapse of psychoanalysis, as well as being loathe to uproot himself from the city in which he had lived since 1860, particularly when he was already dying. But political time was running out more swiftly than Freud's mortality. Beginning her analysis in the spring of 1933, the modernist poet H.D. (Hilda Doolittle) was obsessed that the clinical work would be 'broken by death'; it was not Freud's health that preoccupied her, however, but atrocities against the Jews in Berlin and the 'terror of the lurking Nazi menace'.[13] From 1933 Austria was governed under emergency authoritarian laws, used by Chancellor Engelbert Dollfuss to quell an insurrection of the socialists in February 1934 before he himself was assassinated during an attempted Nazi putsch in July. In the current circumstances the Catholic–fascist alliance of Dollfuss's successor, Kurt Schuschnigg, presented itself as the least worst of three evils – 'native fascism we are willing to take in our stride up to a certain point,' Freud wrote to his son Ernst.[14] But under mounting pressure from Germany, Austrian independence proved to be short-lived. On 11 March 1938, through a combination of propaganda, personal pressure from Hitler and the threat of military force, Schuschnigg – who had tried to outmanoeuvre the Germans by ordering a snap plebiscite on Austrian independence – was forced to step down and allow Hitler's forces in; Freud jotted 'Finis Austriae' in his Chronicle. Two days later Hitler signed a new law incorporating Austria as a province of the German Reich.

Repercussions followed remarkably swiftly: waves of violence against Jews, the looting of apartments and shops, and political murders. On 15 March both Freud's own apartment and the psychoanalytic publishing house were searched. John Cooper Wiley, the American consul in Vienna, cabled u.s. secretary of state Cordell Hull, warning: 'Fear Freud, despite age and illness in danger.'[15] And indeed, a week later, Anna Freud was arrested and interrogated at the Gestapo headquarters over supposed political activities, but released again in the evening. Losing no time, Princess Marie Bonaparte and Ernest Jones, drawing on connections in the British Cabinet, stepped in to give the Freuds protection, and to organize permits and funds (vast fees were required for Jews exiting the country) to facilitate their emigration to England. The Freud case even had the ear of President Roosevelt.

Despite dangerous delays and administrative hurdles across the next couple of months, Sigmund Freud, along with Martha and Anna, finally boarded the *Orient Express* to Paris on 3 June 1938, arriving in London three days later. Other family members had been released during May – Minna Bernays, Freud's son Martin and daughter Mathilde Hollitscher – but four of his sisters remained behind in Austria, all of whom perished. Dolfi died of starvation in the Theresienstadt ghetto, and Rosa, Mitzi (Maria) and Pauli were murdered in the camps. Freud had been saved at the last minute to live out the remaining months of his life in security, and with a certain amount of local acclaim, at 20 Maresfield

Front entrance of Berggasse 19, 1938, photograph by Edmund Engelman.

Gardens in Hampstead (now the site of the Freud Museum London). But it was hardly a time for comfort – as he recounted bitterly in a letter to the weekly review *Time and Tide*:

> After seventy-eight years of assiduous work I had to leave my home, saw the Scientific Society I had founded, dissolved, our institutions destroyed, our printing Press ('Verlag') taken over by the invaders, the books I had published confiscated or reduced to pulp, my children expelled from their professions.[16]

In addition Freud was still undergoing further painful medical procedures (including surgery to the tumour, and treatments with X-rays and radium). The last comment entered in his 'Shortest Chronicle' on 25 August 1939 was one word: *Kriegspanik* (war panic). He died at 3 a.m. on 23 September, two days after his physician, Max Schur, by agreement began administering the morphine that would send him into a painless coma.

Provocations

Over the course of the final fifteen years of his life, Freud and his
work were increasingly internationally feted – he was paired with
Einstein as one of the greatest modern intellectuals and was in
frequent touch with luminaries such as Thomas Mann, Stefan
Zweig, H. G. Wells and Romain Rolland. In the mid-1920s movie
mogul Sam Goldwyn had attempted to pick Freud's brain as 'the
greatest love specialist in the world',[17] and in the later 1930s Freud
reported to Jones that several publishers had approached him to
write a psychoanalysis of the Bible. To honour him on his eightieth
birthday Britain granted him membership of the Royal Society of
Medicine, and a memorial plaque was put up at his birthplace in
Příbor, Moravia. But despite the international acclaim, Freud was
never able to accept that he had finally made his mark. He remained
convinced that the message of psychoanalysis had been received
only at the expense of abandoning its core discoveries. In 1934 he
confided to Arnold Zweig: 'let us make no mistake, this day and
age has rejected me and all I had to give, and acclamations will not
cause it to revise its judgment. Probably my time will come but,
I might add, for the moment it is past.'[18]

We could read in this sense of rejection the weariness of old
age or the effects of physical suffering, or see it as a response to
the many devastating losses that darkened his final decade. Yet
something else is at stake in the severity of Freud's late style that
was much more of his own making, and more akin to a refusal.
Freud did not 'go gently into that good night', nor, it seems, did he
intend for psychoanalysis to cease to be radical, non-conformist
and to a certain extent – and to the chagrin of some of his
colleagues – heretical, even as it was becoming more international
and more legitimate. It is as if Freud was keen to ward off his
assimilation into the world of contemporary psychology with
a final, even grander, set of provocations than those originally

developed in his work on hysteria, sexuality and dreams.

There is not space in this final chapter to consider the many interventions or revisions to existing theories that Freud continued to provide right up until his last moments – psychoanalysis for him remained (as he never ceased to remind his interlocutors) not a finished accomplishment but a work in progress. I will, however, foreground three influential late provocations, all of which engage the question of religion – as if Freud felt that it was here that he wanted his final battles to be fought, to protect analysis from the priests, as he put it. As late as 1937 he would write to his French colleague René Laforgue that it was not the Nazis he was afraid of: 'Help me rather to combat my true enemy . . . the Roman Catholic Church.'[19] The first two of these provocations – 'The Future of an Illusion' and *Civilization and Its Discontents* – were written just two years apart, in 1927 and 1929, and can to a certain extent be dealt with together, as they both focus on the problem of human suffering, and the way in which societies have ensnared themselves in various delusions as compensation.

Both texts share the same bleak underlying social premise, which over the course of the twentieth century has resonated with right-leaning and neo-conservative thinkers (the political theorist Leo Strauss read Freud alongside Machiavelli and Nietzsche) even as Freud's psychoanalytic model was mobilized repeatedly by clinicians and cultural and political theorists of the left (Wilhelm Reich, Herbert Marcuse, Marie Langer). Human relations, for Freud, are ultimately predatory and only slightly evolved from an underlying animal condition that preserves such instinctual wishes as 'incest, cannibalism and lust for killing'.[20] Communities may have found ways to co-operate to extract wealth from the earth, but civilization has grown primarily as a system of regulation imposed on an unwilling majority by a minority 'which understood how to obtain possession of the means of power and coercion'.[21] In *Civilization and Its Discontents*, Freud seemingly went out of his way to offend Christian sensibilities by dismissing its 'proudest claim', that one should 'love thy neighbour'. 'I must honestly confess', he countered, 'that he has more claim to my hostility and even my hatred.'[22] The Christian injunction merely disavowed the reality that the neighbour tempts fellow humans to 'satisfy their aggressiveness on him, to exploit his capacity for work without compensation, to use him sexually without his consent, to seize his possessions, to humiliate him, to cause him pain, to torture and to kill him.'[23]

Of the two essays, 'The Future of an Illusion', though hardly an optimistic text, adopts a more polemical tone in the tradition of Enlightenment materialism and atheism. Positioning religion – like neurosis – as a hurdle in the path of maturity, Freud focuses on how it developed as a response to the experience of helplessness before a hostile natural environment. Drawing on an infantile prototype characterized by parental attachments, primitive society treated adversity as a quasi-human force that could be begged, bribed or appeased: 'the terrifying impression of helplessness in childhood aroused the need for protection . . . which was provided by the father; and the recognition that this helplessness lasts throughout life made it necessary to cling to the existence of a father, but this time a more powerful one.'[24] The whole thing is 'so patently infantile, so foreign to reality', as he remarked dismissively in *Civilisation and Its Discontents*. In 'The Future of an Illusion' he noted that religion generates not only obsessional restrictions, exactly as a neurosis, but a 'disavowal of reality' such as is found only in forms of psychosis.[25] Freud's rather measured conclusion in the earlier text is that it may be true humans cannot bear much reality, but even so they must turn from religion to science to create ever better adaptations to the world and more reliable forms of security.

Civilisation and Its Discontents is a more complex and capacious text, full of memorable metaphors; but it is also much darker, driven less by confidence in the possibility of scientific progress and instead focused on the intractable question of aggression and the psychical turmoil caused by the death drive: 'there are difficulties attaching to the nature of civilization which will not yield to any attempt at reform.'[26] One of Freud's most eloquent themes is human unhappiness: all humans strive after happiness, 'they want to become happy and to remain so,' but there is no possibility at all of this project being carried through.[27] The stumbling block is the inborn mutual hostility and cruelty of human beings, on account of which civilized society is perpetually threatened with disintegration.

One way of dealing with negativity is to direct it inwards: 'the price we pay for our advance in civilization is a loss of happiness through the heightening of the sense of guilt.'[28] But the text also attends to the intricate mechanisms through which people avoid this outcome, notably through forms of intoxication or by deflecting their destructiveness onto external groups. 'It is always possible to bind together a considerable number of people in love,' Freud famously observed, 'so long as there are other people left over to receive the manifestations of their aggressiveness.' He once termed this the 'narcissism of minor differences', which sets up feuds between adjoining communities – North and South Germans, English and Scots – but the turbulence of the late 1920s also conjured up more virulent exercises in group hatred: it was no 'unaccountable chance' that 'the dream of a Germanic world-dominion called for antisemitism as its complement'.[29]

Freud's late texts on society and religion are particularly illuminating for their readings of contemporary politics as a set of attempts to bind the unstable psychical life of groups. 'The Future of an Illusion' targeted the cultural narcissism of German nationalism as well as prohibition in America, which deprived people of alternative stimulants while controlling them through an excess of moralizing piety, while *Civilization and Its*

Discontents presents the psychological premises of communism as themselves 'an untenable illusion'.[30] The 'wildest revolutionaries no less passionately than the most conformist pious believers' were in search of the one thing psychoanalysis refused to offer: consolation.[31] And yet, by the mid-1930s, by which point Freud had lived through a succession of putsches from both the Republican Guard and the Austrian Nazis, he was in somewhat of a quandary, given that the Catholic, right-wing and antisemitic Christian Socials appeared to him to be the only force in Austria capable of keeping the Nazis at bay.

It was in this precarious context that Freud began to construct his third 'heresy', *Moses and Monotheism*, which proved the most taxing for Freud and the most perplexing for contemporary and subsequent readers. At this critical juncture in the fate of the Jews across Central Europe, Freud responded to the renewal of antisemitic persecution with ever more categorical identifications of himself as a Jew. In 1926 he declared that he had 'never lost the feeling of solidarity with my people'; in 1930, he had 'never repudiated his people' and felt 'in his essential nature a Jew'.[32] And yet the fundamental premises of the new work – not only that Moses was an Egyptian, but that he had been murdered by his own chosen people – seemed almost designed to cause offence specifically to Jews, as its opening gambit acknowledges: 'To deprive a people of the man whom they take pride in as the greatest of their sons is not a thing to be gladly or carelessly undertaken, least of all by someone who is himself one of them.'[33]

The main argument, set out in three interlinked and overlapping essays, and supported, like *Totem and Taboo*, by a number of marginal or speculative theories in the contemporary scholarship and analogies drawn from psychoanalytic work, is that Moses, rather than a Hebrew baby set afloat in a basket discovered by the pharaoh's daughter, was born an Egyptian prince (or priest) – the exposure myth was thus an elaboration designed to turn him into a Jew retrospectively. Moses' career is associated with the reign of Pharaoh Amenophis IV (Akhenaten), who imposed on the Egyptians the religion of Aten, replacing the country's myriad deities with a single god, the sun, worshipped as a symbol of radiant truth and justice – the first 'strict monotheism . . . in the history of the world'.[34] After Akhenaten's death, the new religion was repudiated and Egypt reverted to its former plural and magical gods, but – this was Freud's contention – Moses escaped, taking with him an oppressed Semitic people whom he chose to be the torch-bearers of the now proscribed idea of a universal and more abstract deity. In an extra twist, Freud drew on the biblical scholar Ernst Sellin's hypothesis that Moses had been killed by the tribe he had freed from Egypt, who rebelled against the strictures of the new religion and soon abandoned it. To this he added the Egyptologist Edward Meyer's suggestion that 'Moses' conflated two different figures – one who led the Jews out of Egypt, and a second figure belonging to a later period when the Jews had settled in the Midianite region, on the northwest coast of the Arabian peninsula.

This second Moses was instrumental in the adoption of a new deity, the local volcano god Yahweh, identified by its terrifying pillars of fire and smoke. And yet some memory of the original monotheism was retained – whether through an illicit oral tradition, or somehow in the unconscious of the people. As with the murder of the primal father in *Totem and Taboo*, which the Moses text leans on heavily, what was originally violently rejected and destroyed, gradually, secretly, reasserts itself over time, re-emerging after centuries to reshape the Yahweh religion into conformity with the original monotheistic idea. In the long run, it made no difference that the people rejected the teaching of Moses and killed him; his message, routed through a traumatic episode and thrust into the unconscious – just 'like a regular trauma of early childhood' in a neurotic individual – ended up establishing itself all the more completely and compulsively.[35]

The book is a tangled weave, full of tenuous links and arbitrary methodological assumptions that would fail to satisfy biblical scholars, Jewish historians, anthropologists of religion and psychoanalysts themselves. Though there were some who admired Freud's audacity – including H. G. Wells and Einstein – the philosopher Martin Buber found it 'regrettable' and 'based on groundless hypotheses',[36] while others saw in it an attack on Jewish national ideals, even an expression of 'Jewish self-hatred'.[37] It is certainly a text that set itself an impossible task at an impossible time – to both identify and not identify with Judaism; to reassert an icon of Jewish leadership and undermine it; to rewrite the origin story of the Jews while affirming neither their faith nor their nationhood.

Freud was also tormented with misgivings about calling down the wrath of the authoritarian Catholic government in power in Austria, which accounts for the disjointed structure of the text and interrupted rhythm of its publication – drafted in 1934 and reworked in 1936, with the first two parts published in 1937 but the third and longest essay withheld until Freud was in England (the complete work was published in English and German only in 1939). For this reason – and following Freud's assertion that the work, as often as it was laid aside, returned to haunt him 'like an unlaid ghost'[38] – *Moses* has attracted countless interpretations in terms of Freud's 'unconscious' motives, which are assumed phantasmagorically to underpin the twists, turns and hesitations of its manifest argument. Freud was himself frequently identified with Moses by psychoanalytic followers and patients, and biographers have read in it a metaphor for the founding of psychoanalysis itself, or a final flaring of the Oedipal conflict first set out so lucidly in *The Interpretation of Dreams*. As Freud reminds us in *Moses*: 'a hero is someone who has had the courage to rebel against his father and has in the end victoriously overcome him.'[39]

And yet there are more overt rationales one can read it for. First, Freud's *Moses* reinforces the thesis of *Totem and Taboo* regarding the birth of conscience and religion in the killing of the primal father, thereby synchronizing the Judaic tradition to the narrative of Oedipus. In that sense, it attempts a final reiteration of the 'nuclear' thesis of psychoanalysis on a grand historical scale. Indeed, many key ideas from across Freud's career make their curtain call here: the dream-work, parricidal wishes, trauma theory, sexual latency, the compulsion to repeat and the return of the repressed. Second, Freud develops an intriguing account of what it means to read history psychoanalytically, and to be alert to the way events are transmitted intergenerationally in oblique and distorted forms. The Mosaic religion did not vanish without leaving a memory trace; it was subject to tendentious unconscious influences which 'mutilated and amplified it'.[40] Something of this question – how to recover a traumatic history that is structured by forms of repression, denial and forgetting – has been employed by more contemporary scholars working on the history of the Holocaust itself.

Third, in a daring reversal of antisemitic codes, *Moses* both dislocates Judaism from an identification with racial inheritance (the Jews are given their religion by an outsider) and, in defiance of the antisemitic tropes that associated Jewishness with irrationality and degeneracy, makes the Jewish religion itself into the prototype for Western rational enlightenment. In particular, the ban Moses introduced on graven images meant that sensory perception was given second place to abstract cognition: 'a triumph of intellectuality over sensuality'.[41] A Jewish medical psychology, then, would be one that, repeating the original gesture of early Semitic monotheism, had abandoned 'myths, magic and sorcery' in order to establish the basis of secular reason.[42] In that sense, Freud provided not only a revised origin story for Jewish identity, but one for the rational and scientific commitments of psychoanalysis as well. Indeed, in a major textbook of 1945, *The Psychoanalytic Theory of Neurosis*, this is precisely how Otto Fenichel would present analysis, as 'a definite step toward the aim of scientific thinking in psychology – away from the magical'.[43]

What is also clear is that Freud identified his contemporary moment – his exile, his impending death, the abolition of psychoanalysis and the persecution of his followers ('Psychoanalysis', he wrote poignantly in a Prefatory Note to the third section of *Moses*, 'still possesses no home that could be more valuable for it than the city in which it was born and grew up')[44] – with the historic destruction of the Second Temple in Jerusalem in 70 CE. In response the rabbi Yohanan ben Zakkai had asked permission to open the first Torah school in exile and 'from that time on, the Holy Writ and intellectual concern with it were what held the scattered people together.'[45] Freud inserted this example of the 'dematerialization of God' in favour of abstract intellectual culture within the text of *Moses*, but also invoked it as a direct analogy to psychoanalysis at the final Board meeting of the Vienna Psychoanalytic Society on 13 March 1938, commenting 'We are going to do the same.'[46] As the historian of Jewish culture Yosef Yerushalmi noted: suddenly, 'the fate of psychoanalysis had intertwined directly with the actual fate of the Jewish people.'[47]

Alternative Endings

We have considered three different endings so far – Freud's illness, his exile and his *Moses* – each converging on the same quiet sunlit room in North London in 1939, as if this story found its limit in Freud. But there are alternative endings that stem from the same interwar period yet lead beyond Freud into the broader narrative of the twentieth century – Freud's legacy, as it were, began long before his death. By the mid-1920s the impetus driving those first followers who had pledged their loyalty to the Freudian movement was beginning to founder. Karl Abraham died unexpectedly in 1925, while Otto Rank's publications of the early 1920s – particularly *The Trauma of Birth*, which, in prioritizing the birth trauma, introduced major modifications into psychoanalysis

– marked a growing rift with more orthodox colleagues. Though Freud for a while strove to mediate the differences, Rank eventually broke with psychoanalysis and pursued his own therapeutic line in Paris and the United States. Ferenczi also predeceased Freud, in 1933, but not before a cooling in their intimacy as the former became more absorbed in therapeutic experiments of his own – such as a mutuality, or reciprocity, in analysis – recorded for posterity in his radically creative 'Clinical Diary' of 1932, which suffered its own trauma history of repression and neglect before emerging in the 1980s and exerting significant influence on contemporary psychoanalysis.

But a new generation of psychoanalysts, those who staffed the first training institutes and clinics in the immediate post-war period, was just coming into its own, including Anna Freud, Helene Deutsch and Wilhelm Reich in Vienna, Otto Fenichel, Ernst Simmel, Karen Horney and Franz Alexander in Berlin, as well as Melanie Klein, who relocated from Budapest to Berlin in 1921, and then to London in 1926. It is hard to draw a line between where Freud's work ends and their (often eventually quite independent, even oppositional) initiatives begin. The approach of many of these younger analysts was certainly moulded by Freud, but typically by his later model. Rather than beginning with hysteria, dreams and libido, the frame of reference was destructiveness besides sexuality (with much attention paid to aggression and guilt), and a more holistic focus on the three constituents of the psyche – the id, ego and superego – with a new weight falling in particular on the ego as the fulcrum of the personality.

Freud's unfinished 'Outline of Psychoanalysis', drafted in exile, conceived of analytic knowledge as restoring to the ego 'its mastery over lost provinces of [its] mental life', as if it were the beleaguered capital of a dismembered Habsburg empire of the mind.[48] The next generation took up the gauntlet of further investigating the ego as a complex structure in its own right – capable of splitting itself, and with an armoury of defences at its disposal, enumerated in Anna Freud's classic work of 1936, *The Ego and the Mechanisms of Defence*. For Franz Alexander – who in the early 1930s took up a university chair in psychoanalysis in Chicago – Freud's work on the ego ushered in a new era, one less preoccupied with interpreting unconscious symptoms and more with systematizing observations on the 'total personality',[49] while Heinz Hartmann's *Ego Psychology and the Problem of Adaptation*, originally lectures for the Vienna Psychoanalytic Society in 1937, set its sights on an emergent general theory of human behaviour. 'Ego psychology' was to become the meeting ground between psychoanalysis, non-analytic psychology, education, mental health and the social sciences, a vision that meshed with the more expansive social democratic outlook of interwar Vienna and Berlin.

In addition, this younger generation incorporated Freud's late reorientation of his account of anxiety. For much of his career Freud had asserted that repressed sexual impulses returned to haunt consciousness in the guise of anxiety (this had shaped his earlier reading of phobias). But in 1926, partly in response to Rank, he wholly revised this idea: anxiety, he now judged, was essentially a reaction to an anticipated situation of danger that had originally been generated by an external threat such as fear of castration, or the separation from a loved object. The ego remobilized its earliest traumatic experiences of helplessness in subsequent situations in order to trigger defence mechanisms – systemic forms of avoidance – whenever such danger threatened to re-emerge. Thus anxiety now generated repression, rather than the other way around. The new perspective once more reinforced the focus on the ego, which now scanned the internal and external environment for signals of danger, an approach that facilitated connections between psychoanalysis and ethology.

It is here, during the later 1930s, that one of the most significant trajectories for psychoanalysis in the twentieth century took shape, partly as a result of the persecution in Europe that sent waves of Jewish and politically vulnerable analysts – nearly two hundred in all – to New York, Boston, Los Angeles and elsewhere in the United States, where they tried to rebuild their lives and their clinical practice.[50] Here they were forced to integrate themselves with a more medically oriented framing of psychoanalysis, which Freud had resisted in Vienna. Some, like Erich Fromm and Karen Horney, took up a more dissident 'Neo-Freudian' position, rejecting the core emphasis on universal instincts in favour of exploring cultural variability and the impact of social environment, but were marginalized in the profession. However, the ego psychologists, particularly those committed to integrating Freud's theories with medical and developmental approaches, found their stock rising in the United States and were able to play up the emphasis on biology that had re-emerged in some of Freud's later works (his *New Introductory Lectures* of 1933 and the 'Outline' deploy terms such as 'innate disposition' or 'somatic organization' with a frequency hardly seen since the early pre-psychoanalytic phase of his career).

At the same time, American involvement in the Second World War massively foregrounded the importance of psychodynamic work on anxiety and trauma, as the explosion of war-related neuroses (around 850,000 u.s. soldiers were in treatment) gave the chance to demonstrate the efficacy of psychoanalytic therapeutic techniques.[51] The rise of psychiatrists sympathetic to psychoanalysis to key wartime positions had a knock-on effect in post-war planning for programmes of mass mental health care. The major inroads Freudians made into psychiatry, coupled with a new political investment in mental health reform per se, created the conditions for an enormously successful expansion of psychoanalysis in North America between the 1940s and the 1970s.

I cannot here adequately present all the dimensions of this flourishing of psychoanalytic influence, which stretched from

Poster for *Freud: The Secret Passion* (1962, dir. John Huston), a drama based on Freud's life.

child guidance, social work, counselling and criminology to Cold War social science, conservative and utopian political theory, popular psychology, literature, cinema and the arts, and even religion. Suffice to say that by the early 1950s psychoanalysts, though still relatively few in number, were fast becoming an elite profession, taking lead positions in many psychiatric clinics and teaching hospitals (by the early 1970s half of psychiatrists in American general psychiatry were psychoanalytic specialists).[52] Psychoanalysis became for a while the linchpin of a mid-century promise of a 'sane' society, to be found in the advertising of Madison Avenue, in Dr Spock's best-selling manual on baby care, at the core of New York intellectual Lionel Trilling's 'Liberal Imagination', Bruno Bettelheim's accounts of autism and Erik Erikson's of the mid-life crisis. Betty Friedan, writing in the early 1960s, deplored the way in which 'Freudian and pseudo-Freudian theories settled everywhere, like fine volcanic ash.'[53]

Ultimately, it was the medical success story that paved the way for psychoanalysis' fall from grace during the 1970s and '80s. By hitching Freud's more diverse and humanistic project to a narrower, more positivistic ideal of psychiatric science, and by promising definitive interventions across so many areas of mental health psychology, psychoanalysis rendered itself vulnerable to attack as it was increasingly unable to compete with the emerging fields of psychopharmacology and neuroscience, precisely on the grounds of testable experimental methods and scientific accountability. Psychoanalysis was thus ousted from American psychiatry during the 1980s amid a wave of critiques and denunciations – its costliness, its failure to develop adequate research methods, and its *sui generis* conceptualization of mental processes. In some sense, it has been falling from scientific grace ever since, although not entirely: in fact, the literature of the past decade shows a growing number of psychiatrists and psychologists renewing advocacy for psychodynamic approaches and the 'talking cure' as necessary complements to the short-term cognitive therapies and drugs that had displaced it across much medical practice, particularly as a tool for dealing with depression, anxiety, and somatic or eating disorders across the longer term.

But the mainstream American story and the medicalized version of psychoanalysis is only one version of how Freud's later theoretical revisions were extended. A quite different account emerges if one looks to the debates around gender and sexuality that erupted in the 1920s when Freud and others began to address a blind spot in his theorization of sexuality – specifically feminine development and female desire ('the sexual life of adult women is a "dark continent" for psychology,' he acknowledged in 1926).[54] In a number of short, revisionary papers of the mid-1920s, Freud took his rather unitary model of the Oedipus complex and began to pay more attention to the distinction between the sexual identities of boys and girls. Interestingly, for Freud, this had no biological basis – for a while children of either sex were oblivious to anatomical difference, all moving from an original orally centred state of being, through an 'anal' stage in which they became more invested in control over the boundaries of their body, and entering a 'phallic' phase still assuming that each sex and both parents bore a penis.

It was at this point, in Freud's new version, that boys and girls were struck by a traumatic recognition – not so much a distinction between male and female, but between having a male genital and being castrated. For the incipient male child, this perceived threat of losing the phallus inaugurates a 'castration complex' through which the boy revokes his exclusive attachment to the mother, and to his own desire, and finds a way out of danger by identifying with the threatening paternal agency, in this way internalizing the rule of social authority. Girls, instead, while still cleaving to the idea that they too possess a phallus, are struck by the visible inferiority of their own organ and fall victim to 'penis envy' – 'She has seen it,' he wrote notoriously in 1925, 'and knows that she is without it and wants to have it.'[55] From this moment, according to Freud, the developing woman carries a wound to her narcissism, like a scar; she abandons her wish for a penis and her attachment to her mother, instead taking her father as a love object, with the ambition of one day gaining a child as a replacement for the missing organ. In a further paper on 'Female Sexuality' from 1931, Freud added that she may instead respond with a revulsion towards sexuality, or 'cling with a defiant self-assertiveness to her threatened masculinity', but only by desiring the father will she find her way to the 'normal female attitude'.[56]

Freud's new model provoked criticisms from the growing number of female psychoanalysts, though, interestingly, it was not the concept of penis envy that was objected to, but rather the masculine bias of the terms in which a woman's destiny was framed. For Helene Deutsch in Vienna, the boy's discovery of his phallus was matched, perhaps eventually outflanked, by the girl's accession to an equally valuable psychological possession of a vagina, through which she could not only confer on her eventual male partner the possibility of a metaphorical return to the womb but recollect that state within herself in the creation of another life. For Karen Horney in Berlin, reproductive capacity gave the woman an indisputable 'physiological superiority', reflected in the boy's 'intense envy of motherhood'. A woman's sexual identity could only have been represented to herself as inferior by virtue of the male gaze by which it was mediated: the psychology of women representing 'a deposit of the desires and disappointments of men'.[57] In fleeing womanhood girls were responding as much to the actual social subordination of women as to their own desire. This is only scraping the surface of a rich and varied debate, but notably both these authors reacted against Freud's account by centralizing motherhood in female desire.

When second-wave feminism erupted in the 1970s, such images of women as failed or castrated men were more than ripe for demolition. But what drew the ire of critics such as Kate Millett, Betty Friedan and others was not entirely Freud's own theorization of sexual identities, but the way it had been mobilized across American psychiatric psychoanalysis and pop psychology to confirm the heteronormative and patriarchal edifice of contemporary American society. Indeed, one outcome of the renewed energetic debates between feminism and psychoanalysis was eventually to recover the radicalism of some of Freud's original assertions concerning the precarity and variability of gender identity and sexual desire. Perhaps it was precisely as Freudian theory was released from the grip of mainstream psychiatry that it was able to inform a flourishing new literature on gender, sexual desire and queer identities from the 1980s onwards, in the work of theorists such as Leo Bersani, Judith Butler, Jacqueline Rose and Lee Edelman, while psychoanalysts such as Julia Kristeva, Juliet Mitchell and Jessica Benjamin in turn provided new and more complex reframings of the dialectical emergence of desire and subjective and sexual embodiment.

These are just some of the stories that take off from the 1920s and '30s, producing complex intellectual trajectories across the century and into the present day. Others could include the distinctive traditions unfolding in Britain through the work of Melanie Klein, Anna Freud and Donald Winnicott, centring on parent–infant relations. Their practice was heavily inflected by the experience of the Second World War: Winnicott, a psychoanalyst and paediatrician, worked with child evacuees and from the mid-1940s onwards gave advice to young mothers through a series of radio broadcasts; Anna Freud set up the Hampstead War Nursery, and later a child therapy clinic, still functioning today, which has developed into an international hub for outcomes research on child development and mental well-being. Klein and Winnicott developed psychoanalysis into a theory of 'object relations' – the internalized emotional bonds operating between children and mothers, whose absence, presence or intensity becomes crucial within later functioning – and an ideology of care that found a strong resonance in the early post-war discourse of the welfare state. A different narrative again is provided by the radically original initiatives of the psychiatrist Jacques Lacan in Paris, beginning in the 1930s and flourishing as a post-war 'return to Freud', drawing on an entirely different set of influences – French Surrealism, Hegelian philosophy, and eventually linguistics and mathematical topology – and exerting a strong influence over French intellectual culture of the 1960s and '70s, including the work of Julia Kristeva, Françoise Dolto, Cornelius Castoriadis and Louis Althusser (alongside Michel Foucault and Jacques Derrida, Lacan became one of the key post-structuralist theorists of the relation between the subject and 'discourse'). A further story could be told by beginning with Wilhelm Reich's and Erich Fromm and Max Horkheimer's studies of fascism and authority in the 1930s, running through the work of Theodor Adorno, Herbert Marcuse and other critical theorists who combined Freud and Western Marxism in their analyses of totalitarian society, and whose work resonates in contemporary analyses of demagoguery, neo-fascism and mass politics.

Just as Freud's star was waning in 1980s psychiatry, it was rising elsewhere in new forms that remain active today – whether in the social sciences and humanities in academia, or as an influence in psychotherapeutic practices and psychodynamic models of mental health worldwide. The story of Chinese psychoanalysis was truncated with the founding of the People's Republic in 1949 but is now re-emerging as part of an intensive 'psycho-boom', generating a Freud for the twenty-first century. As the hundred-year anniversaries of various Freud texts have come around one by one, his ideas have not seemed dead and buried; rather, they continue to provide useful tools for interpreting the present. But how much such present-day projects can still be ascribed to Freud, how present he is in such later developments, is a matter of judgement. The continuing – and expanding – domain of psychotherapy, for instance, now represents a blend of different traditions, and certainly no longer stands or falls with Freud, nor is it entirely rooted in his original insights, even if some of his terms and ideas remain ubiquitous across the field.

Perhaps two distinguishing features stand out as specifically Freudian in contemporary work. If psychoanalysis is the science of the disowned parts of the self – whether this is traumatic histories, narcissistic disavowals, neurotic symptoms or repressed sexuality and aggression – it is no surprise that it remains enduringly heretical. In a recent survey of the future of psychoanalysis in the academy, Michael Rothberg, who teaches comparative literature and Holocaust and trauma studies at UCLA, saw in it 'a hermeneutic of suspicion that we need today to make sense of our world', while the critical theorist Anna M. Parkinson, based at Northwestern University, found in it 'keen tools for thinking through – and learning to tolerate – that which is paradoxical, ambiguous, a-normative, and ambivalent'.[58] Such responses are replicated across the world touched by Freud's work. In its specific attention to that which is concealed, disowned, disavowed or threatening, psychoanalysis is an approach and practice that still retains the power to disturb, complicate and make us see things differently, and which therefore continues to spawn disbelief and counter-accusations, detractors as well as agitators.

The second is more basic, and perhaps more persistently connected to Freud's name and his project. It goes back to a declaration in his final 'Outline of Psychoanalysis':

We know two kinds of things about what we call our psyche (or mental life): firstly, its bodily organ and scene of action, the brain (or nervous system) and, on the other hand, our acts of consciousness, which are immediate data and cannot be further explained by any sort of description. Everything that lies between is unknown to us.[59]

Conscious life, in which we feel relatively at home and through which we orient ourselves in our daily interpersonal encounters, surely does not emerge fully formed from the brain, like Athena from the head of Zeus in the classical myth. There are intermediary layers between bodily impulses and mental perceptions, a substrate to consciousness – and not just a neurological one, but a psychological substrate, a domain in which thinking is formed, but also screened, dreamed or deflected, so that thought reaches us consciously only after some quite specific siftings, detours and elaborations: the thoughts we are capable of thinking. It is in this gap that Freud posited first the unconscious, and then the id, the superego and the defensive processes of the ego. A place that exists categorically – *everything that lies between is unknown to us* – as well as being, by definition, the place we are least comfortable addressing, accepting or cognizing.

Freud knotted together a therapy, a psychology, a theory of the emotions, a practice of self-observation, and an understanding of social, cultural and moral life. And he did so around complex principles that were distinctively 'psychical' – or psychoanalytic – and which cannot be reduced to other disciplinary frameworks of experimental psychology, philosophy of mind, neurobiology or psychiatry. Simply put, his topic was the nature of our unconscious mental life, and the narratives and obsessions that take hold within it. This is another reason why psychoanalysis – as a discipline, an approach, a practice – is here to stay. It will endure for as long as our obsessions, our anxieties, our wishes. Is Freud dead? In Rio, London, New York, Chicago and Los Angeles, Berlin, Paris, Moscow, Budapest, Jerusalem, Montreal, Helsinki, Santiago, Kolkata, Beirut, Johannesburg – even Vienna – you wouldn't know it.

References

Abbreviations

F-FL   Jeffrey Moussaieff Masson, ed., *The Complete Letters of Sigmund Freud to Wilhelm Fliess, 1887–1904* (Cambridge, MA, 1995)

F-J   William McGuire, ed., *The Freud/Jung Letters: The Correspondence Between Sigmund Freud and C. G. Jung* (Princeton, NJ, 1974)

FLOT   Peter Gay, *Freud: A Life for Our Time* (London, 1989)

FMC   Ronald W. Clark, *Freud: The Man and the Cause* (St Albans, 1982)

LSF   Ernst L. Freud, ed., *Letters of Sigmund Freud* (New York, 1992)

LWSF   Ernest Jones, *The Life and Work of Sigmund Freud*, 3 vols (New York, 1953–7)

SE   Sigmund Freud, *The Standard Edition of the Complete Psychological Works of Sigmund Freud*, ed. James Strachey and Anna Freud, 24 vols (London, 1953–74)

Introduction: The Freudian Aftershock

1 *F-J*, p. 86, p. 88.

2 *SE* XVII, p. 248.

3 Attributed to Jorge Luis Borges. See Jacques Alain-Miller, 'Enigmatized Coitus: A Reading of Borges' [1997] (2006), www.lacan.com; and Otto Gross, *Selected Works, 1901–1920* (Hamilton, NY, 2012), p. 257.

4 Spielmayer, quoted in *LWSF*, vol. II, p. 124; William Stern in Anthony Kauders, 'Truth, Truthfulness, and Psychoanalysis: The Reception of Freud in Wilhelmine Germany', *German History*, XXXI/1 (March 2013), p. 7; Ernst Kretschmer, quoted in *LWSF*, vol. III, p. 11.

1 Histories, 1856–84

1 Sigmund Freud, Letter to Arnold Zweig, 31 May 1936, in *The Letters of Sigmund Freud and Arnold Zweig*, ed. Ernst L. Freud (New York, 1970), p. 127.

2 Steven Beller, *Vienna and the Jews, 1867–1938* (Cambridge, 1989), p. 122.

3 *SE* IV, p. 193.

4 Quoted in Beller, *Vienna and the Jews, 1867–1938*, p. 151.

5 Steven Beller, 'Class, Culture and the Jews of Vienna, 1900', in *Jews, Antisemitism and Culture in Vienna*, ed. Ivar Oxaal, Michael Pollak and Gerhard Botz (London, 1987), p. 48.

6 Marsha Rozenblit, *The Jews of Vienna, 1867–1914: Assimilation and Identity* (Albany, NY, 1983), p. 123.

7 Anna Freud Bernays, 'My Brother Sigmund Freud', *American Mercury*, LI/203 (November 1940), p. 336.

8 Emil du Bois-Reymond, *Jugendbriefe an Eduard Hallmann*, ed. Estelle du Bois-Reymond (Berlin, 1918), p. 108.

9 Walter Boehlich, ed., *The Letters of Sigmund Freud to Eduard Silberstein, 1871–1881* (Cambridge, MA, 1990), p. 142.

10 Ibid., p. 70.

11 *LWSF*, p. 92.

12 Dennis B. Klein, *Jewish Origins of the Psychoanalytic Movement* (New York, 1981), p. 10.

13 *SE* IV, p. 197.

14 *SE* XX, p. 9.

15 Beller, *Vienna and the Jews, 1867–1938*, p. 205.

16 *LWSF*, p. 101, p. 33.

17 Ibid., p. 26.

18 *SE* XX, p. 9.

19 Albrecht Hirschmuller, *The Life and Work of Josef Breuer: Physiology and Psychoanalysis* (New York and London, 1989), p. 28; Klein, *Jewish Origins of the Psychoanalytic Movement*, p. 11.

20 *LWSF*, p. 127.

21 *SE* IV, p. 441.

22 Ibid., p. 442.

23 Ibid.

24 Ibid., p. 196.

25 Ibid., p. 197.
26 Franz Brentano, *Psychology from an Empirical Standpoint* (London, 1995), p. 102.
27 Ibid., p. 103.
28 *SE* III, p. 310.
29 Ibid., p. 322. Italics in original.
30 *SE* IV, p. 17.
31 Ibid., p. 190.
32 Ibid., p. 12.
33 Ibid., p. 20.
34 Ibid., pp. 424–5.
35 Ibid., p. 425.
36 Ibid., p. 553.
37 Ibid., p. 191.
38 Ibid., p. 250.
39 Ibid., p. 251.
40 Ibid., p. 255.
41 *F-FL*, p. 268.
42 *SE* IV, p. 132.
43 Ibid., p. 160.
44 Ibid., p. 467.
45 Ibid., p. 330.
46 Ibid., p. 208.
47 Ibid., p. 214.
48 Ibid., p. 216.
49 Ibid.
50 Carl Schorske, *Fin-de-Siècle Vienna: Politics and Culture* (London, 1980), p. 196.
51 *SE* IV, p. 469.
52 *LWSF*, p. 89.
53 Ibid., p. 91.

2 Memories, 1885–95

1 *SE* II, p. 7.
2 Andrew Scull, *Hysteria: The Disturbing History* (Oxford, 2011), p. 107.

3 *SE* III, pp. 16–17.

4 *SE* II, p. 4.

5 Scull, *Hysteria*, p. 54.

6 *SE* III, p. 19.

7 J.-M. Charcot, *Clinical Lectures on the Diseases of the Nervous System* (London, 1991), vol. III, p. 12.

8 *SE* III, p. 20.

9 Axel Munthe, *The Story of San Michele* (London, 1930), pp. 302–3.

10 *SE* III, p. 16.

11 *LWSF*, p. 145.

12 Andreas Mayer, *Sites of the Unconscious: Hypnosis and the Emergence of the Psychoanalytic Setting* (Chicago, IL, 2013), p. 125.

13 *LWSF*, p. 23.

14 Ibid., p. 75.

15 *LWSF*, vol. I, p. 298.

16 Élisabeth Roudinesco, *Freud in His Time and Ours* (Cambridge, MA, 2016), p. 50.

17 *LWSF*, vol. I, p. 230.

18 Elaine Showalter, *The Female Malady: Women, Madness and English Culture, 1830–1980* (London, 2004), p. 121; Scull, *Hysteria*, p. 100.

19 *SE* II, p. 13.

20 Ibid., p. 21.

21 Ibid., p. 155.

22 *F-FL*, p. 73, p. 158.

23 Showalter, *The Female Malady*, p. 135.

24 *F-FL*, p. 44.

25 Ibid.

26 Ibid., p. 57, p. 77.

27 Ibid., p. 130.

28 Ibid., pp. 81–2.

29 Ibid., p. 108.

30 Ibid., p. 109.

31 Ibid., p. 110.

32 Mayer, *Sites of the Unconscious*, p. 112, p. 129.

33 *F-FL*, p. 17.

34 *LWSF*, vol. I, p. 261.

35 *SE* II, p. 48.

36 Ibid., pp. 49–50.
37 Ibid., p. 84.
38 Ibid., p. 24.
39 Ibid., p. 25.
40 Ibid., p. 22.
41 Ibid., p. 29.
42 Ibid., p. 30.
43 Ibid., p. 31.
44 Ibid., p. 7.
45 Ibid., pp. 33–4.
46 Ibid., p. 6.
47 Ibid., p. 160.
48 Ibid., p. 8.
49 Ibid., p. 209.
50 Ibid., p. 211.
51 Ibid., p. 67.
52 Ibid., p. 12.
53 Ibid., p. 269.
54 *F-FL*, p. 145.
55 *SE* II, p. 288.
56 Ibid., p. 108.
57 Ibid., p. 63.
58 Ibid., p. 265.
59 Ibid., p. 271.
60 Ibid., p. 289.
61 Ibid., p. 272.
62 *F-FL*, p. 129.
63 Ibid., p. 146.
64 Ibid., p. 152.
65 *SE* III, p. 219.
66 Adam Phillips, *Becoming Freud: The Making of a Psychoanalyst* (New Haven, CT, 2014).
67 Showalter, *The Female Malady*, p. 162; *LWSF*, vol. I, p. 278.
68 *SE* III, p. 192.
69 *SE* IV, p. 107.
70 Ibid., p. 106.

3 Dreams, 1896–1901

1 *F-FL*, p. 261.
2 *SE* IV, p. xxvi.
3 *SE* III, p. 199.
4 Ibid., p. 153.
5 Ibid., p. 203.
6 Ibid., p. 201.
7 *F-FL*, p. 238.
8 Ibid.
9 Ibid., p. 239.
10 Norman Kiell, ed., *Freud Without Hindsight: Reviews of His Work, 1893–1938* (Madison, CT, 1988), p. 68.
11 *F-FL*, p. 202.
12 Ibid., p. 261.
13 Ibid., pp. 230–31.
14 Ibid., p. 249.
15 Ibid., p. 284.
16 Ibid., p. 264.
17 Ibid., p. 250.
18 Ibid., p. 272.
19 Ibid., p. 311, p. 342.
20 Ibid., p. 345.
21 *SE* IV, p. 128.
22 *F-FL*, p. 417.
23 *SE* IV, p. 215.
24 Ibid., p. 111.
25 Ibid., p. 91.
26 Ibid., p. 4.
27 Ibid., pp. 196–8.
28 Ibid., p. 218.
29 Ibid., p. 603.
30 Ibid., p. 567.
31 Ibid., p. 294.
32 *SE* VIII, p. 165.
33 *SE* IV, p. 323.
34 *SE* VI, p. 80.

35 *SE* IV, p. 279.

36 Ibid., p. 293.

37 Ibid.

38 Ibid., p 160.

39 Ibid., p. 583.

40 Ibid., p. 97.

41 Ibid., p. 583.

42 Ibid., p. 99, p. 312, p. 277.

43 Lydia Marinelli and Andreas Mayer, *Dreaming by the Book: Freud's 'The Interpretation of Dreams' and the History of the Psychoanalytic Movement* (New York, 2003), pp. 18–19.

44 Kiell, *Freud Without Hindsight*, p. 128; on the reattribution to Emma Eckstein, see Marinelli and Mayer, *Dreaming by the Book*, p. 48.

45 Kiell, *Freud Without Hindsight*, p. 120.

46 Virginia Woolf, Letter to Saxon Sydney-Turner, 3 February 1917, in *The Question of Things Happening: The Letters of Virginia Woolf*, vol. II: *1912–1922* (London, 1976), p. 141; Lytton Strachey, 'According to Freud', in *The Really Interesting Question* (London, 1972), pp. 113–14.

47 Lou Andreas-Salomé, *The Freud Journal* (London, 1987), p. 48.

48 *F-FL*, p. 394.

49 Ibid., p. 402.

50 Ibid., p. 412.

51 Eva Brabant, Ernst Falzeder and Patrizia Giampieri-Deutsch, *The Correspondence of Sigmund Freud and Sándor Ferenczi*, vol. I: *1908–1914* (Cambridge, MA, 1993), p. 221.

4 Desires, 1902–10

1 *SE* XVI, p. 303.

2 *SE* X, p. 176.

3 *FLOT*, p. 178.

4 *SE* VII, pp. 7–8.

5 Ibid., p. 28.

6 Ibid., p. 44.

7 *SE* XI, p. 75.

8 *F-FL*, p. 433.

9 Arnold I. Davidson, *The Emergence of Sexuality: Historical Epistemology and the Formation of Concepts* (Cambridge, MA, 2001), p. 60.

10 Philippe Van Haute and Herman Westerink, 'Introduction', in Sigmund Freud, *Three Essays on the Theory of Sexuality: The 1905 Edition* (London, 2016), p. xviii.

11 Michel Foucault, *The History of Sexuality: An Introduction* (Harmondsworth, 1987), p. 36.

12 *SE* VII, pp. 147–8.

13 Ibid., p. 139.

14 Ibid., p. 150.

15 Ibid., pp. 151–2.

16 Ibid., p. 160.

17 Ibid., p. 189.

18 Ibid., p. 181.

19 Ibid., p. 186.

20 Ibid., p. 192.

21 Ibid., p. 232.

22 Ibid., pp. 171–2.

23 *FMC*, p. 191.

24 Ibid., p. 234.

25 *F-J*, pp. 196–7.

26 Ibid., p. 95.

27 Ibid., p. 218.

28 Ernest Jones, *Free Associations* (New Brunswick, NJ, 1990), p. 181.

29 Ernst Falzeder, ed., *The Complete Correspondence of Sigmund Freud and Karl Abraham, 1907–1925* (London, 2002), p. 38.

30 Richard Skues, 'Clark Revisited: Reappraising Freud in America', in *After Freud Left: A Century of Psychoanalysis in America*, ed. John Burnham (Chicago, IL, 2012), p. 65.

31 *SE* XX, p. 52.

32 Eva Brabant et al., *The Correspondence of Sigmund Freud and Sándor Ferenczi*, vol. I: *1908–1914* (Cambridge, MA, 1993), p. 156.

33 George Makari, *Revolution in Mind: The Creation of Psychoanalysis* (London, 2008), p. 252.

34 *F-J*, p. 373, p. 259.

35 Ibid., p. 376.

36 *SE* X, p. 7.

37 Ibid., p. 65.
38 Ibid., p. 72.
39 *F-J*, p. 199.
40 *SE* X, p. 42.
41 Ibid., p. 99.
42 Ibid., p. 122.
43 *F-J*, p. 251.
44 *SE* X, p. 158.
45 Ibid., p. 201.
46 Ibid., p. 163.
47 Ibid., p. 245.

5 Mythologies, 1910–23

 1 *SE* XXII, p. 211.
 2 *SE* IX, p. 152.
 3 *F-J*, pp. 251–2.
 4 Lydia Marinelli and Andreas Mayer, *Dreaming by the Book: Freud's 'The Interpretation of Dreams' and the History of the Psychoanalytic Movement* (New York, 2003), p. 57.
 5 *SE* XVII, p. 97.
 6 *SE* XII, p. 17 (quoting the doctor's report).
 7 Ibid. (quoting the doctor's report).
 8 Ibid., p. 13 (quoting Schreber).
 9 Ibid., p. 71.
10 *F-J*, p. 427.
11 *SE* XII, p. 82.
12 *SE* XIV, p. 91.
13 Ibid., pp. 74–5.
14 Ibid., pp. 89–91.
15 Ibid., p. 94.
16 Ibid., p. 61.
17 *F-J*, p. 459.
18 *SE* XIII, p. 233.
19 Carl Jung, *Psychology of the Unconscious* (London, 1922), p. 82.
20 Ibid., p. 84.

21 Ibid., p. 81.

22 *F-J*, p. 515.

23 *SE* XIV, p. 62.

24 *F-J*, p. 539.

25 *SE* XIII, p. 1.

26 Ibid.

27 Ibid., p. 4.

28 Ibid., p. 17.

29 Ibid., p. 18.

30 Ibid., p. 27.

31 Ibid., pp. 31–2.

32 Ibid., p. 66.

33 Ibid., p. 89.

34 Ibid., p. 141.

35 Ibid., pp. 141–2.

36 Ibid., p. 143.

37 Ibid.

38 Ibid., pp. 141–2.

39 Ibid., p. 10, p. 81, p. 53.

40 Ibid., p. 46, p. 96.

41 *SE* XIV, p. 195.

42 Ibid., p. 276.

43 See Erik Linstrum, 'Spectres of Dependency: Psychoanalysis in the Age of Decolonization', in *Psychoanalysis in the Age of Totalitarianism*, ed. Matt ffytche and Daniel Pick (London, 2016).

44 *SE* XVII, p. 104.

45 *SE* XIII, p. 157.

46 *SE* XIV, pp. 275–80.

47 *LWSF*, vol. II, p. 192.

48 *FLOT*, p. 351.

49 Ibid., pp. 278–80.

50 Ibid., p. 286.

51 Ibid., p. 297.

52 Ibid., p. 7.

53 *SE* XXII, p. 115.

54 Sigmund Freud and Lou Andreas-Salomé, *Letters*, ed. Ernst Pfeiffer (New York, 1985), p. 32.

55 *SL*, p. 312, p. 319.

56 *FLOT*, p. 377.

57 Stefan Zweig, *The World of Yesterday* (London, 2009), p. 305.

58 Letter to Katá Levy, June 1923, *LSF*, p. 344.

59 *FMC*, p. 385.

60 Perry Meisel and Walter Kendrick, eds, *Bloomsbury/Freud: The Letters of James and Alix Strachey, 1924–1925* (London, 1986), pp. 28–9.

61 *SE* XVII, p. 167.

62 *LWSF*, vol. III, p. 31.

63 *SE* XIX, p. 19.

64 *SE* XIII, p. 138.

65 *SE* XIV, p. 251.

66 *SE* XVIII, p. 16.

67 Ibid., p. 23.

68 Ibid., p. 27.

69 Walter Benjamin, 'The Storyteller', in *Illuminations: Essays and Reflections* (New York, 1969), p. 84.

70 *SE* XVIII, p. 36.

71 Ibid., p. 38.

72 Ibid., p. 50.

73 *FLOT*, p. 397; *LWSF*, vol. III, pp. 274–5.

74 *SE* XIV, pp. 278–9.

75 *SE* XVIII, p. 73.

76 Ibid., p. 90.

77 Ibid., p. 94.

78 Ibid., p. 95.

79 Ibid., p. 77.

80 Ibid., p. 123.

81 Ibid., p. 80.

82 Ibid., p. 124, p. 127.

83 *SE* XIX, p. 23.

84 Ibid., p. 31.

85 Ibid., p. 53.

86 *SE* XVII, p. 143.

87 *SE* XIX, p. 56.

6 Heresies, 1924–39 and After

1 Freud's remark to a sculptor who commented on his looking cross, quoted in *FMC*, p. 487.

2 *SE* XXIII, p. 219.

3 Ibid., p. 216.

4 Ibid., p. 243.

5 *SE* XX, p. 187.

6 Élisabeth Roudinesco, *Freud in His Time and Ours* (Cambridge, MA, 2016), p. 339, p. 382.

7 *FLOT*, p. 640.

8 *SE* XXIII, p. 216.

9 Michael Molnar, trans., *The Diary of Sigmund Freud, 1929–1939* (London, 1992), p. 9, p. 17.

10 *FMC*, p. 490.

11 *FLOT*, p. 616.

12 Carl Jung, 'The State of Psychotherapy Today', in *Collected Works*, vol X: *Civilization in Transition* (New York, 1964), p. 165.

13 H.D., *Tribute to Freud* (New York, 2012), p. 140.

14 *LSF*, p. 420.

15 *FLOT*, p. 623.

16 *SE* XXIII, p. 301.

17 *FMC*, 461.

18 Ernst L. Freud, ed., *The Letters of Sigmund Freud and Arnold Zweig* (New York, 1970), p. 59.

19 *FMC*, p. 491.

20 *SE* XXI, p. 10.

21 Ibid., p. 6.

22 Ibid., p. 110.

23 Ibid., p. 111.

24 Ibid., p. 30.

25 Ibid., p. 74, p. 43.

26 Ibid., p. 115.

27 Ibid., p. 76.

28 Ibid., p. 134.

29 Ibid., pp. 114–15.

30 Ibid., p. 49.

31 Ibid., p. 145.

32 *SL*, p. 365; *SE* XIII, p. 15.

33 *SE* XXIII, p. 7.

34 Ibid., p. 20.

35 Ibid., p. 50; *SL*, p. 439.

36 *FLOT*, p. 646.

37 Trude Weiss-Rosmarin, quoted in Yosef Hayim Yerushalmi, *Freud's Moses: Judaism Terminable and Interminable* (New Haven, CT, 1991), p. 113.

38 *SE* XXIII, p. 103.

39 Ibid., p. 12.

40 Ibid., p. 43.

41 Ibid., p. 113.

42 Ibid., p. 24.

43 Otto Fenichel, *The Psychoanalytic Theory of Neurosis* (New York, 1996), p. 4.

44 *SE* XXIII, p. 55.

45 Ibid., p. 115.

46 *LWSF*, vol. III, p. 221.

47 Yerushalmi, *Freud's Moses*, p. 16.

48 *SE* XXIII, p. 173.

49 Franz Alexander, *Psychoanalysis of the Total Personality* (New York, 1935).

50 Eli Zaretsky, *Secrets of the Soul: A Social and Cultural History of Psychoanalysis* (New York, 2004), p. 276.

51 Ibid., p. 280.

52 Nathan G. Hale Jr, *The Rise and Crisis of Psychoanalysis in the United States: Freud and the Americans, 1917–1985* (Oxford, 1995), p. 246.

53 Betty Friedan, *The Feminine Mystique* (New York, 1964), p. 115.

54 *SE* XX, p. 212.

55 *SE* XIX, p. 252.

56 Karen Horney, 'The Flight from Womanhood: The Masculinity-Complex in Women, as Viewed by Men and by Women', *International Journal of Psychoanalysis*, VII (1926), pp. 330, 326.

57 *SE* XXI, pp. 229–30.

58 Zahid Chaudhary et al., 'What Is the Future of Psychoanalysis in the Academy?', *Psychoanalysis and History*, XX/1 (2018), pp. 28–9.

59 *SE* XXIII, p. 144.

Further Reading

Texts by Sigmund Freud

The following works can be found in Sigmund Freud, *The Standard Edition of the Complete Psychological Works of Sigmund Freud*, ed. J. Strachey and A. Freud, 24 vols (London, 1953–74):

Studies on Hysteria (with Joseph Breuer) (1893–5), *SE* II
'The Aetiology of Hysteria' (1896), *SE* III
The Interpretation of Dreams (1900), *SE* IV–V
The Psychopathology of Everyday Life (1901), *SE* VI
'Fragment of an Analysis of a Case of Hysteria [Dora]' (1905), *SE* VII
Three Essays on the Theory of Sexuality (1905), *SE* VII
'Creative Writers and Day-Dreaming' (1908), *SE* IX
'Analysis of a Phobia in a Four-Year-Old Child [Little Hans]' (1909), *SE* X
'Notes upon a Case of Obsessional Neurosis [The Rat Man]' (1909), *SE* X
'Formulations on the Two Principles of Mental Functioning' (1911), *SE* XII
Totem and Taboo (1912–13), *SE* XIII
'Mourning and Melancholia' [1915] (1917), *SE* XIV
'From the History of an Infantile Neurosis [The Wolf Man]' (1918), *SE* XVII
'The Uncanny' (1919), *SE* XVII
Beyond the Pleasure Principle (1920), *SE* XVIII
Group Psychology and the Analysis of the Ego (1921), *SE* XVIII
'The Ego and the Id' (1923), *SE* XIX
'Inhibitions, Symptoms and Anxiety' (1926), *SE* XX
Civilization and Its Discontents (1930), *SE* XXI
'An Outline of Psycho-Analysis' [1938] (1940), *SE* XXIII

Correspondence

Brabant, Eva, Ernst Falzeder and Patrizia Giampieri-Deutsch, eds,
    The Correspondence of Sigmund Freud and Sándor Ferenczi, 3 vols
    (Cambridge, MA, 1993–2000)

Freud, Ernst L., ed., *The Selected Letters of Sigmund Freud* (New York, 1992)

McGuire, William, ed., *The Freud/Jung Letters: The Correspondence Between
    Sigmund Freud and C. G. Jung*, trans. Ralph Manheim and R.F.C. Hull
    Freud (Cambridge, MA, 1988)

Masson, Jeffrey Moussaieff, ed., *The Complete Letters of Sigmund Freud to
    Wilhelm Fliess, 1887–1904* (Cambridge, MA, 1995)

Pre-Psychoanalytic Background

Crabtree, Adam, *From Mesmer to Freud: Magnetic Sleep and the Roots of
    Psychological Healing* (New Haven, CT, 1993)

Ellenberger, Henri, *The Discovery of the Unconscious: The History and
    Evolution of Dynamic Psychiatry* (London, 1970)

ffytche, Matt, *The Foundation of the Unconscious: Schelling, Freud and the
    Birth of the Modern Psyche* (Cambridge, 2012)

Hirschmüller, Albrecht, *The Life and Work of Josef Breuer: Physiology and
    Psychoanalysis* (New York and London, 1989)

Klein, Dennis B., *Jewish Origins of the Psychoanalytic Movement* (Chicago, IL,
    1985)

Makari, George, *Revolution in Mind* (London, 2008)

Mayer, Andreas, *Sites of the Unconscious: Hypnosis and the Emergence of the
    Psychoanalytic Setting*

Ritvo, Lucille B., *Darwin's Influence on Freud: A Tale of Two Sciences* (New
    Haven, CT, 1990)

Schorske, Carl, *Fin-de-Siècle Vienna: Politics and Culture* (London, 1980)

Showalter, Elaine, *The Female Malady: Women, Madness and English Culture,
    1830–1980* (London, 2004)

About Freud and His Work

Anzieu, Didier, *Freud's Self-Analysis* (Madison, CT, 1986)

Appignanesi, Lisa, and John Forrester, *Freud's Women* (London, 2000)

Bernheimer, Charles, and Claire Kahane, eds, *In Dora's Case: Freud – Hysteria – Feminism* (New York, 1990)

Clark, Ronald W., *Freud: The Man and the Cause* (London, 1982)

Danto, Elizabeth Ann, *Freud's Free Clinics: Psychoanalysis and Social Justice, 1918–1938* (New York, 2005)

Edmundson, Mark, *The Death of Sigmund Freud* (London, 2007)

Flem, Lydia, *Freud the Man: An Intellectual Biography* (New York, 2003)

Fletcher, John, *Freud and the Scene of Trauma* (New York, 2013)

Forrester, John, *Dispatches from the Freud Wars: Psychoanalysis and Its Passions* (Cambridge, MA, 1997)

——, *Thinking in Cases* (Cambridge, 2017)

——, and Laura Cameron, *Freud in Cambridge* (Cambridge, 2017)

Freud, Ernst L., Lucie Freud and Ilse Grubrich-Simitis, eds, *Sigmund Freud: His Life in Pictures and Words* (New York, 1976)

Gardiner, Muriel, ed., *The Wolf-Man and Sigmund Freud* (London, 1972)

Grinstein, Alexander, *Sigmund Freud's Dreams* (New York, 1980)

Grosskurth, Phyllis, *The Secret Ring: Freud's Inner Circle and the Politics of Psychoanalysis* (London, 1991)

H.D., *Tribute to Freud* (New York, 2012)

Jones, Ernest, *The Life and Work of Sigmund Freud*, 3 vols (New York, 1953–7)

Lear, Jonathan, *Freud* (Abingdon, 2015)

Lohser, Beate, and Peter M. Newton, *Unorthodox Freud: The View from the Couch* (New York, 1996)

McGrath, William J., *Freud's Discovery of Psychoanalysis: The Politics of Hysteria* (Ithaca, NY, 1986)

Marinelli, Lydia, and Andreas Mayer, *Dreaming by the Book: Freud's 'The Interpretation of Dreams' and the History of the Psychoanalytic Movement* (New York, 2003)

Molnar, Michael, *Looking Through Freud's Photos* (London, 2015)

Phillips, Adam, *Becoming Freud* (New Haven, CT, 2014)

Ricoeur, Paul, *Freud and Philosophy: An Essay on Interpretation* (New Haven, CT, 1970)

Rose, Louis, *The Freudian Calling: Early Viennese Psychoanalysis and the Pursuit of Cultural Science* (Detroit, MI, 1998)

Roudinesco, Élisabeth, *Freud in His Time and Ours* (Cambridge, MA, 2016)

Solms, Mark, and Michael Saling, eds, *A Moment of Transition: Two Neuroscientific Articles by Sigmund Freud* (London, 1990)

Spankie, Ro, *Sigmund Freud's Desk: An Anecdoted Guide* (London, 2019)

Sulloway, Frank J., *Freud: Biologist of the Mind* (New York, 1979)

Wollheim, Richard, *Freud* (London, 1971)

Wortis, Joseph, *Fragments of an Analysis with Freud: A First-Hand Account* (New York, 1954)

Yerushalmi, Yosef H., *Freud's Moses: Judaism Terminable and Interminable* (New Haven, CT, 1991)

Beyond Freud

Bar-Haim, Shaul, *The Maternalists* (Philadelphia, PA, 2021)

Bosteels, Bruno, *Marx and Freud in Latin America: Politics, Psychoanalysis, and Religion in Times of Terror* (London and New York, 2012)

Etkind, Alexander, *Eros of the Impossible: The History of Psychoanalysis in Russia*, trans. Noah Rubins and Maria Rubins (Boulder, CO, 1997)

Fanon, Frantz, *Black Skin, White Masks* (London, 1986)

ffytche, Matt, and Daniel Pick, eds, *Psychoanalysis in the Age of Totalitarianism* (London, 2016)

Frosh, Stephen, *The Politics of Psychoanalysis: An Introduction to Freudian and Post-Freudian Theory* (New Haven, CT, 1987)

——, *Key Concepts in Psychoanalysis* (London, 2002)

Fuechtner, Veronika, *Berlin Psychoanalytic: Psychoanalysis and Culture in Weimar Republic Germany and Beyond* (Berkeley, CA, 2011)

Hale, Nathan G. Jr, *The Rise and Crisis of Psychoanalysis in the United States*, 2 vols (Oxford, 1995)

Herzog, Dagmar, *Cold War Freud: Psychoanalysis in an Age of Catastrophes* (Cambridge, 2017)

Jacoby, Russell, *The Repression of Psychoanalysis: Otto Fenichel and the Political Freudians* (New York, 1983)

Kurzweil, Edith, and William Phillips, *Literature and Psychoanalysis* (New York, 1983)

Laplanche, J., and J.-B. Pontalis, *The Language of Psychoanalysis* (London, 1988)

Mitchell, Juliet, *Psychoanalysis and Feminism* (Harmondsworth, 1975)

Mitchell, Stephen A., and Margaret J. Black, *Freud and Beyond: A History of Modern Psychoanalytic Thought* (New York, 1995)

Phillips, Adam, *Winnicott* (London, 1988)

Plotkin, Mariano Ben, *Freud in the Pampas: The Emergence and Development of a Psychoanalytic Culture in Argentina* (Stanford, CA, 2001)

Roudinesco, Élisabeth, *Jacques Lacan and Co.: A History of Psychoanalysis in France, 1925–1985* (Chicago, IL, 1990)

Segal, Hanna, *Klein* (Glasgow, 1979)

Shakry, Omnia El, *The Arabic Freud: Psychoanalysis and Islam in Modern Egypt* (Princeton, NJ, 2017)

Shapira, Michal, *The War Inside: Psychoanalysis, Total War, and the Making of the Democratic Self in Postwar Britain* (Cambridge, 2013)

Whitebook, Joel, *Freud: An Intellectual Biography* (Cambridge, 2017)

Zaretsky, Eli, *Secrets of the Soul: Social and Cultural History of Psychoanalysis* (New York, 2004)

Zhang, Jingyuan, *Psychoanalysis in China: Literary Transformations, 1919–1949* (Ithaca, NY, 1992)

Acknowledgements

It has been a pleasure to be immersed for some years in Freud's prodigious, testing and always surprising body of work. I encountered him first as a student of literature – Freud the interpreter – then later as the theorist of modern subjectivity. Over the last ten years I have been increasingly drawn to the therapeutic dimensions of his work – its value for navigating the puzzling and distressing aspects of human contact.

There will never be a definitive account of Freud, and the current work is my best attempt to locate the meaning of his achievement at this point in time, amid the multiplicity of voices, influences and developments radiating outwards from his life and writings. In this task I have been above all indebted to Andrea Brady, my partner, for many years of critical discussions, jokes and poesis concerning Freud, dreams, the unconscious, and all the riddles of loving, thinking and relating. I am also indebted to the children, Hannah, Ayla, Abel and Marlow, who had to tolerate my absence and my presence, and who quip that I have been reading the same book on holiday for years, by Sigmund 'Frood'.

In terms of completing this work, I am deeply grateful for the opportunity to have spent 2018–19 as a Resident Associate at the National Humanities Center – a shiny modernist cube of humanities hive-work in the pollen-rich treescape of North Carolina – where part of this book was drafted, and to the Department of Psychosocial and Psychoanalytic Studies at the University of Essex for supporting this research and providing a disciplinary home for psychoanalytic work in the academy.

My heartfelt thanks also go to Dagmar Herzog, Daniel Pick, Dany Nobus, Michael Molnar and Shaul Bar-Haim for their support and encouragement over many years, and for being excellent readers and annotators of the text. Likewise to the members of the History of Psychoanalysis Research Group at Essex, who read drafts of some of the chapters, and to an indefinable host of mentors, collaborators, colleagues, interlocutors, graduate students and discussants who have helped define my Freud, or the Freudian me. To name some of them here, my thanks go out to Sally Alexander, Dominic Angeloch, Manuel Batsch, Louise Braddock, Felicity Callard, Marco Conci, Karl Figlio, Stephen Frosh, Bob Hinshelwood, Tom Kugler, Carolyn Laubender, Kevin Lu, Sarah Marks, Andreas Mayer, Nikolay Mintchev, Leonardo Niro, Rebecca Reynolds, Michael Roper, Jacqueline Rose, Sonu Shamdasani, Keston Sutherland, Lyndsey Stonebridge, Barbara Taylor, Helen Tyson and Julie Walsh. I would also like to thank all the past students on the MA Psychoanalytic Studies at the University of Essex who over many years have helped me to think through and to re-evaluate the meaning of Freud's work in a contemporary context.

Finally, I want to thank Reaktion Books – in particular Ben Hayes, for originally commissioning this book, my editors Michael Leaman and Amy Salter and picture editor Alex Ciobanu for their patience and assistance, particularly during the drawn-out pandemic year of work.

Photo Acknowledgements

The author and publishers wish to express their thanks to the below sources of illustrative material and/or permission to reproduce it:

Album/Alamy Stock Photo: pp. 62, 168; akg-images: p. 17; Chronicle/ Alamy Stock Photo: pp. 23, 55, 59, 92, 112, 162, 181; duncan1890/iStock. com: p. 46; Everett Collection Historical/Alamy Stock Photo: p. 164; © Freud Museum London: pp. 6, 21, 85, 87, 101, 108, 111, 135, 184, 189; © Galton Collection, University College London (CC BY-NC-SA 3.0): p. 99; courtesy Ilmari Karonen: p. 73; Imagno/Hulton Archive via Getty Images: p. 67; from Fortunato Indovino, *Il vero mezzo per vincere all'estrazione de' lotti* . . . (Venice, 1809), photo courtesy Special Collections, Princeton University Library, NJ: p. 81; from *Kikeriki*, XIII/40 (18 May 1873): p. 27; courtesy Lewis Walpole Library, Yale University, New Haven, CT: p. 105; Musée d'histoire de la médecine, Université Paris V – René Descartes: p. 53; from George Nicol (attrib.), *An Hour at Bearwood: The Wolf and the Seven Kids* (London, 1838), photo courtesy Special Collections, Toronto Public Library, ON: p. 145; from Dr Paul Richer, *Études cliniques sur l'hystéro-épilepsie ou grande hystérie* (Paris, 1881), photos courtesy Lamar Soutter Library, UMass Medical School, Worcester, MA: p. 52; Rijksmuseum, Amsterdam: p. 13; Wellcome Collection, London (CC BY 4.0): pp. 20, 124, 132.